Teaching Kids to
Think Critically

Teaching Kids to Think Critically

Effective Problem Solving and Better Decisions

Clifton Chadwick

ROWMAN & LITTLEFIELD
Lanham • Boulder • New York • London

Published by Rowman & Littlefield
A wholly owned subsidary of The Rowman & Littlefield Publishing Group, Inc.
4501 Forbes Boulevard, Suite 200, Lanham, Maryland 20706
www.rowman.com

16 Carlisle Street, London W1D 3BT, United Kingdom

British Library Cataloguing in Publication Information Available

Library of Congress Cataloging-in-Publication Data
Chadwick, Clifton B.
Teaching kids to think critically : effective problem-solving and better decisions
/ Clifton Chadwick.
  pages cm
  ISBN 978-1-4758-1065-3 (cloth : alk. paper) — ISBN 978-1-4758-1066-0 (pbk. :
alk. paper) — ISBN 978-1-4758-1067-7 (electronic) 1. Critical thinking—Study
and teaching. 2. Problem solving—Study and teaching. 3. Reasoning—Study
and teaching. I. Title.
  LB1590.3.C385 2014
  370.15'2—dc23   2014019035

Printed in the United States of America

To my lovely daughter, Josephine Noor, who is quickly
learning inferences and critical thinking,
And,
To my lovely granddaughter, Florencia, who will
soon start to learn to think critically.

Contents

ONE

Introduction

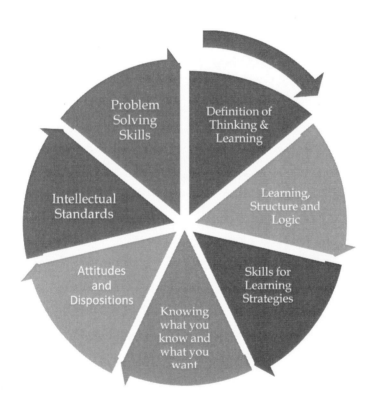

Teaching our children how to be effective thinkers should be one of our highest priorities along with teaching them to be ethically and morally solid. The modern world requires that people become more and better thinkers in order to respond to and help shape the information-rich world in which we live. I think all parents want their children to be high-quality thinkers (see figure 1.1).

1

Think about it. Why would you want your children to be able to think at a highly effective level? Could they just think like everyone else and have a simple life? Is that even possible anymore? Should they just let other people worry about the important problems in life and then do whatever the other people do? Should they adopt situational ethics and go with the flow?

Let us start with one important observation. Most children do not learn to think in school. I know that sounds controversial, but it is true. Schools mostly teach encyclopedic information that they call "education." In one well-known research study, the author[1] found that the thinking skills of children in 12th grade were basically the same skills they had in fourth grade.[2] I am not kidding. I know this may be hard to believe.

In our research, we have studied schools that claim to the highest heavens that they are dedicated to teaching thinking (after all, it is the rage). The principals, the department heads, and the teachers all said that teaching thinking is a very high priority for them. But when we do systematic classroom observation to see what teachers actually do, we find that they do almost nothing to stimulate thinking—sad but true. Of course, children do have to learn a lot of information, much knowledge. But the issue is not only to memorize the information but also to learn how to use it. And the persons who can most influence a child's desire to think are not teachers but parents. A child's curiosity and inclination to search, question, and solve starts very early, and it is parents who typically kick off the desire to think, not teachers.

During the history of modern education, only a rather small portion of students was expected to learn to think critically. In the 18th and 19th centuries, only people who would become leaders, members of clergy, philosophers, and business leaders were those who should learn much information and learn how to think critically and analytically in order to solve problems, to lead people, to develop sound businesses, and to do medical and other research. Most people received little or no education.

At the beginning of the 20th century, the industrial revolution and the manufacturing process began to require workers who knew basic information and had simple skills. Thus, the public school curriculum became reading, writing, and arithmetic—the three Rs. The schools were seen as places where a teacher—who knew the subjects and relevant information—would show and tell students what they should know and what they should learn.

Education was a teacher-centered enterprise in a rather factory-like setting. All students got basically the same exposure to the same contents for the same amount of time and with the same form of evaluation of learning in a fundamentally passive situation where they sat in rows and tried to absorb (memorize) what the teacher was saying. Since they were all being treated the same (time, form, and content), the primary difference in results in learning was a function of talent, intelligence, and economic situation.

Schools taught but they also selected—they identified and encouraged the brighter and more persistent students who often came from families that had a better education and more economic resources. For decades, high schools in England, Germany, the United States, and other countries were divided into two streams: the academic stream, which would lead to liberal arts education and the university, and the vocational stream, which would lead students to occupational situations that did not require a university education.

This dual system implicitly said that only certain students required advanced study of analytic and critical thinking. Further, as mentioned above, most schools did not and still do not teach critical thinking in a systematic manner. The teacher-centered classroom is much more attuned to teaching content information, sometimes referred to as "covering the textbook" (which is de facto the curriculum). Conveying information is important, but it is not usually compatible with teaching critical thinking. To a great extent, how schools evaluate what students learn is done by summarizing how much knowledge and how much content they can answer on multiple-choice tests.

Even though conditions in the outside world are changing, the major countries that are considered to be highly successful in education (Singapore, Finland, South Korea, Taiwan, and so on) operate teacher-centered classrooms that emphasize the ability to learn very conservative information-laden curricula.

But there has been a major change in the economic and social environment throughout the world. There has been an information revolution, that is, a major development in the role that information has come to play in the economy of the world. Information has become a major factor in production as well as a commodity or product that is sold in the market. This revolution can be seen as a result of technological advances that have brought about the vast expansion of the capabilities of computers, particularly small ones, allowing significant improvements in the production process and increasing the quality and quantity of goods and services available in the market.

The information age occurred because of microminiaturization, spanning from the advent of the personal computer in the late 1970s to the development of the Internet in the early 1990s and the adoption of that technology by the public in the two decades after 1990. Bringing about a fast evolution of technology in daily life, as well as of educational lifestyle, the information age has allowed rapid global communications and networking to shape modern society.

Not only does the increase in information help productivity, but it also contributes to the development of new consumer products, such as computers, mobile phones, recording devices, video devices, text-reading devices, and applications, including productivity software and games. The revolution has also included significant increases in innovations, patents, and improvements in almost all fields, including magnetic resonance imaging and handheld inventory control devices in supermarkets. Many of these innovations have significantly improved the quality of life for many people. Other innovations have created major distractions (you are not a gadget).

In this new age, jobs traditionally associated with the middle class (assembly line workers, data processors, foremen, and supervisors) are beginning to disappear through either outsourcing or automation. Individuals who lose their jobs must either move up, joining a group of "knowledge workers" (engineers, attorneys, scientists, professors, executives, journalists, or consultants), or settle for low-skill, low-wage service jobs.

The "knowledge workers" form about 20 percent of the workforce, and that percentage is growing. A basic aspect of their work is that they must know how to think analytically and be able to solve problems. They are able to compete successfully in the world market and command high wages. How they work represents a major challenge to the traditional content of heavy teacher-centered education. This information revolution has led to what is called the knowledge economy, characterized by the ability to think analytically and critically to solve problems and create new ideas in all sectors of the economy.

The picture is clear. More than ever before, knowing how to think clearly, logically, and critically is becoming very important. Teaching children to become effective thinkers is being increasingly recognized as an important and immediate goal of education. The world is moving away from mass production toward more and more service and particularly something called the knowledge economy, which means that the new source of production is having information and knowing how to use it to create something worthwhile and valuable. And that requires greater and greater skills in thinking.

One report[3] says that complex communication and expert thinking are rapidly replacing normal cognitive activity (remembering and understanding) and normal manual skills. The future world, this knowledge economy, requires students to be comfortable with abstract ideas and to learn about the creativity required for innovation. If students are to be able to function successfully in a highly technical, knowledge-oriented society, they must be structured with thinking skills and habits of lifelong learning. This is a very different kind of education than what most of us have received and what most of our children are currently receiving.

As information growth has occurred, the world has seen changes in work and employment. For example, there has been a growth in part-time employment and a reduction in full-time employment. Further, knowledge and information have become more important in production than simple labor or manual skills, particularly in new business endeavors. The productive or industrial sectors of the economy are declining, while the service sector is growing. Another trend is that the one-organization career model is becoming more rare, and job mobility and career changes are more common.

Knowledge and know-how are gradually taking the place of buildings and machinery as the most valuable assets of business. The speed at which information can travel and be shared, the sophistication of many modern products and services (particularly technology related), the growing intelligence of the modern consumer who expects top value for the money, and the increasing customization of goods and services to meet peoples' needs are part of this shifting playing field. Competitive advantage derives from the clever application of intellect and knowledge to solve business problems.

Is this being taught in the schools?

Nonroutine interactive skills and nonroutine analytic skills are growing in demand, while routine cognitive and manual skills are declining in importance, a logical result of the information revolution and the knowledge economy (see figure 1.1).[4]

Not only are schools failing to adequately teach critical thinking and complex reasoning, but most universities are also failing to do so. It is

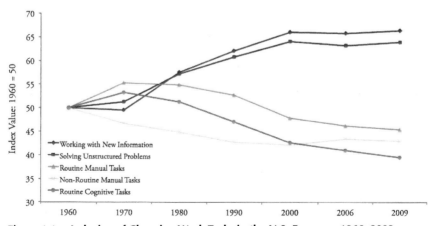

Figure 1.1. Indexing of Changing Work Tasks in the U.S. Economy 1960–2009

widely agreed that these capacities are the foundation for effective democratic citizenship and economic productivity. But recent research has suggested that about half of university students do not improve in critical thinking and that in the other half the overall improvement is slight.[5]

Most important in the new world's information age, thinking skills are crucial for educated persons to cope with a rapidly changing world. Specific subject knowledge, while important, is not as vital as the ability to learn and make sense of and use new information.

These changes have meant that more education is required to compete in the modern economy. Literacy and numeracy continue to be a major part of the core curriculum, but schools are being asked to promote new forms of knowledge, such as the following:

- Metacognitive skills and abilities
- The ability to integrate formal and informal learning
- Discrimination between declarative knowledge (knowing what) and procedural knowledge (knowing how)
- The ability to access, select and evaluate knowledge from an information heavy world
- The ability to create, transpose and transfer knowledge
- The ability to work and communicate as teams
- The ability to locate oneself in the job market, choose and fashion one's needs for relevant education and training

In the field of work, some changes are occurring related to the idea of a knowledge economy. New forms of teamwork are emerging, particularly in some of the service organizations. The ability to manage large amounts of information has made inventory control more efficient and led to more efficient production facilities and just-in-time production systems. Another trend is toward continuous improvement of procedures in the workplace.

From the standpoint of the schools, students' performance on measures of higher-order thinking ability has shown that critical thinking is *not* widespread. Schools teach information, discrete knowledge elements normally called content.[6] They do very little to teach children how to use the content to think. Most students do not score well on measures of their abilities to recognize assumptions, evaluate arguments, and draw and appraise inferences. Many do not even know what an inference is.

For several decades, school systems have been attempting to find new ways to improve the overall achievement of their students. Cooperative learning, use of technology, smaller class sizes, constructivism, higher investments in education, and many other ideas have been put forth. So far, none of these ideas seems to have had any major effect on student achievement (see figure 1.2).

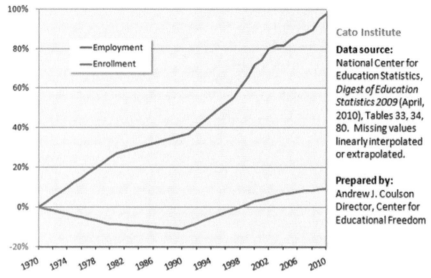

Figure 1.2.   Costs vs. Enrollment Growth

Look at the issue of class size. Over the past 40 years, employment of teachers has increased by 100 percent while student enrollment has increased by only about 10 percent. Total spending on K–12 education has more than doubled in 40 years (adjusted for inflation), while math scores have gone up only about 6 percent and reading scores about 1 percent. This is definitely not a good return on investment.

Since the schools are very slow to catch on to this idea, it is the smart and concerned parents who have to step up to take responsibility and teach their children how to think.

We know why parents must teach their children to think. How is that done?

When someone says, "Talk to them," most parents think you have said something obvious, but that is not the case. Of course, parents talk to their children, but very often they do so at the wrong level. They make declarative and imperative statements, but they do not truly interact. They hear questions and sometimes answer them and sometimes ignore them. When they get a really good "why" question from their child, they often answer, "Because!"

Questions, questions, questions. That is the key to teaching children to think. But not just any questions. Logically organized questions will stimulate children to grasp new information, evaluate it, transform it into something they understand, and gauge it against what they already know.

Parents, particularly mothers, are the people who spend the most time with their children. They have the optimum opportunity to influence their children's thinking. Most mothers do attempt to shape thinking. They read to their children, they talk to them, they answer the child's questions, and they help them shape and grow their vocabulary.

But they could do so much more.

The best way to teach children to think is to ask them questions—questions that are appropriate to the subject and situation in which they are learning and that are also orchestrated around a serious set of criteria that will lead to good thinking. In this book, we explain and illustrate the criteria and how to apply them to help your children learn to think.

My eight-year-old daughter asks me questions all the time. Sometimes she almost drives me up the wall. One day, when she was in the midst of a stream of questions, a friend who was present asked her why she had so many questions. She said, "Because I want to know; I want to know it all." That is what we parents want: curious children who want to know it all. They will become good thinkers if we guide them correctly.

The issue then is how best to guide a young person toward good-quality thinking (see figure 1.3).

The basic way to approach the subject of thinking is to understand the components of thinking, the scheme and idea of what is involved. All of us think, all of the time. Most of us do not think very much about what is involved in thinking. Yet thinking about thinking is the key to good thinking.

To begin, let us discriminate between certain human emotional functions, such as thinking, feeling, and wanting (desiring).

Feeling is evaluating ourselves and responding to our environment, which is usually unconscious. We are happy, sad, depressed, anxious, stressed, calm, worried, excited, eager, and so on, and these states guide our behavior. Feelings are the first line of our relationship with the world: we feel any sense of threat or danger or any need, such as to eat, to drink, or to get out of the cold or the heat. We feel love and affection for those who are close to us; we feel national pride and religious belonging.

Desiring (wanting) means responding to our feelings by setting goals, purposes, agendas, values, and emotions. We desire what presumably

will be best for us, what will satisfy our needs. We desire to satisfy our basic needs, to have a secure and safe environment, and to have a close affiliation with our family and friends and a sense of belonging to a group that represents shared values.

We also desire respect, self-esteem, and confidence as well as some form of creativity, morality, and the ability to solve problems and achieve transcendence. That does not always happen, as often our emotions lead us to do unproductive things, take contrary positions, develop less-than-optimal attitudes, and so on. An example could be the tendency for some students, particularly young girls, to develop a negative attitude toward mathematics.

What is *thinking*? It is making sense of the world. Thought and thinking are mental representations (forms) and mental processes. Thinking allows humans to represent or model the immediate and distal world and deal with it according to goals, plans, ends, and desires. Synonyms of *thinking* include *cognition, consciousness, sentience,* and *imagination.* Note that all of these words have to do with awareness, with metacognition, with being aware of the process and results of thinking.

Critical or effective thinking is that which is focused on deciding what to believe or do, with a disposition to provide evidence in support of one's suggestion or conclusions and to ask for evidence from others before accepting their conclusions. It is the process of determining the authenticity, accuracy, meaningfulness, and value of information. It is the use of those skills and strategies that will increase the likelihood of achieving desired outcomes, as determined by the thinker. It will lead the person to be able to make good career decisions, astute financial decisions, and general life decisions.

Critical thinking is purposeful, reasoned, and normally goal directed. It is thinking that is directed toward solving problems, deducing inferences, calculating probabilities, and making decisions. It is what psychologists call a higher-order skill.

Thinking has components that can be represented in figure 1.4.

Planning is a kind of deciding, which is a kind of reasoning, which is a kind of conceptualizing, which is a kind of thinking. It also involves remembering and reading.

Learning is a product of reasoning. Learning is not an end in itself but a product of the reasoning process that can then be used to successfully operate and respond in one's environment, such as in solving problems. For example, people's representations of categories are influenced by the way they use those categories in problem solving.

Reason is the ability to generate conclusions from assumptions or premises. Reason implies rationality and is closely related to the concepts of language and *logic,* the Greek word that in Latin becomes the root for *reason* (from Latin *logica,* from Greek *logikē,* from the feminine of *logikos,* or reason, i.e., from *logos,* reason). Sometimes, reason is contrasted with emotion, mysticism and superstition, authority, intuition, and faith as a more objective and reliable way to discover what is true.

A reason is a consideration that explains or justifies some concept, idea, or event. Philosophers typically discriminate between explanatory reasons or justifying reasons. Explanatory reasons are thoughts that help explain things that have happened. They may be thought of as "reasons why" events occur. "I am wet because it is raining" (see figure 1.3).

Reason can also be thought of as a cause. For example, a car starts because it has been constructed such that when its ignition is activated by a key, the starter motor initiates the main motor. When we talk about people and reasons, the term *motivation* arises. Jim went to the store to buy groceries. Julie went to school to learn. Josephine went to the piano teacher to learn to play the piano. Buying groceries and learning are the motivating reasons in these cases. When a person is acting rationally, she is motivated by those factors that she believes justify her actions.

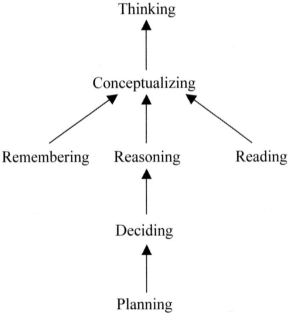

Figure 1.3.   Levels of Thinking

FEELINGS AND THINKING

> since feeling is first
> who pays any attention
> to the syntax of things
> will never wholly kiss you;

—e.e. cummings

Feelings come first. They dominate our behavior. The importance of our feelings is so great that some psychologists have suggested that thinking and feeling are actually different cognitive systems. And feelings, since they are so closely related to survival, obviously dominate.

But rational thinking is or can be a close second: it guides our decisions and helps us choose that which will most likely lead to achieving our goals and desires—usually but not always. One of the primary goals in teaching thinking is to allow and encourage reasoning, particularly logical thinking, to take a more dominant role in the children's lives. That way, thinking comes to control you, your emotions, and your decisions and whether you control your thinking. Controlling thinking is useful and adaptive. For example, it is a good way to reduce impulsive behavior.

Impulsivity is erratic and poorly controlled behavior. Teachers who refer to a student as being impulsive usually invoke images of students who rarely stop to think before they act, who attempt tasks before they fully understand the directions, who often demonstrate remorse when their actions have led to errors or mishaps, who call out frequently in class (usually with the wrong answer), and who have difficulty organizing their materials. Increased metacognition, that is, awareness of thought processes, is an excellent way to reduce impulsivity.

LOGICAL THINKING, CRITICAL THINKING

How do we think? Through perceiving, analyzing, clarifying, determining, comparing, contrasting, synthesizing, and judging. We perceive our world through our senses. We see, hear, smell, feel, and taste aspects of the world. We do the following:

- Determine the degree of accuracy about what we perceive (how real is it?)
- Clarify what we perceive (am I sure that is what I saw?)
- Compare and contrast that with what our past experience has shown us (have I seen this before?)

- Synthesize what we perceive (now I can relate these sights and sounds to others), and then
- Make judgments (this is important but dangerous)

What do we think about? Mostly, we think about ourselves and our immediate environment. That is logical and inevitable. The range of what we think about is also a result of our training, the influences of our parents and family, our relation with our immediate reality, and other factors. For example, if we live in a family that has many books and where reading is important, we will tend to think verbally, while if we live in a family where movies and television are important, we will tend to think visually, that is, using many images. If we live in a small family, we will think differently than if we live in a big family.

The content of thinking is information, ideas, feelings, problems, events, sequences, past and future, cause, change, intentions, anxieties, and identity—just about everything you can imagine.

What do we use to think with? Our sensory impressions (what we see and feel through our senses) are represented and interpreted through images and language—verb constructions, syntax, images, episodes, metaphors, schemes, structures, and representations.

How many forms? To begin with, we think to respond to our environment, then to evaluate, plan, and make decisions. Something happens, and we react. Sometimes we think before we react. Sometimes we do not.

Thinking for the acquisition of new information (for learning) is very important. Since we often (maybe usually) do not know all we need to know, we use thinking to acquire information that will help us evaluate our situation and make decisions and choices. We need to know more about where we are, what we are doing, what is happening to us, and where we are going —good or bad. And the younger we are, the more important is acquisition. Young children require much new information as a fundamental and crucial part of growing up. In part, that is what education is about.

The next step is thinking for analysis. Besides acquiring new information, we have to determine things such as why did it happen (to me), what will happen next, how will it affect me, and what should I do. Thus, thinking is for the consideration of possible consequences, causes, and effects: to evaluate what has happened and to attempt to anticipate what will happen. This is thinking for evaluation. So much of thinking is to evaluate situations so that we can ensure that we have enough information to make good decisions. And this is a controversial area because many decisions are taken reflexively, without enough information.

Many people talk about creative thinking, but it is difficult to describe and difficult to achieve. Still, we offer a few ideas about what parents can do to stimulate creativity in their children.

Educational and psychological research supports the idea that instruction in thinking does improve academic achievement. It also supports the teaching of several specific thinking skills and suggests that certain teaching methods improve thinking skills.

THE FIVE ELEMENTS OF QUALITY THINKING

There are five elements involved in good, logical, critical, and creative thinking (see figure 1.4):

- The skills involved in effective and efficient learning that are often called *cognitive processing strategies*
- The mastery of the *logic and structure* of what is being learned
- *Awareness* of what one knows and does not know, how one knows and how one thinks, and what one wants (dispositions), usually called *metacognition*
- The standards or guidelines for the validity and reliability of what one knows, called *intellectual standards*
- The knowledge and skills involved in *solving problems* in different subjects or domains

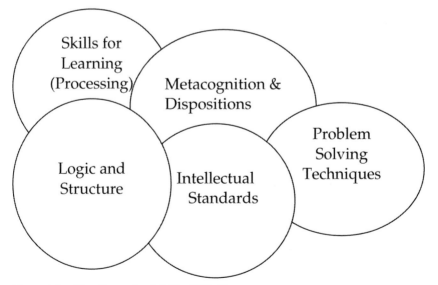

Figure 1.4. Five Elements of Critical Thinking

CONTENT AND STRUCTURE

Thinking is about something. In math, you think about numbers, arrangements, processes, problems, and so on. In science, you think about the
world around you—about systems of classification, methods, processes
and results. In language, you think about (and with) vocabulary, grammar, and syntax. Content is always involved when we think: you cannot
think about nothing. Therefore, the first element that we must pay attention to is how children acquire the content they will use for thinking.

All knowledge has some kind of structure—its basic internal logic. We,
as parents, want to pay attention to two different aspects of the structure:
the logic and structure that underlies the subject or phenomenon and the
structure and logic that our children are developing and constructing in
their minds as they learn. In chapter 2, we look more closely at the concepts of the logic and the structure of knowledge.

COGNITIVE PROCESSING STRATEGIES AND SKILLS

This is a fancy term for effective ways to get new information into the
brain. Often, content is acquired by memorizing things. Sometimes, that
is a good way to learn. But several better ways to learn do exist. Asking
questions, drawing concept maps, studying layouts, comparing and contrasting, using metaphors and analogies, developing inferences, and other
techniques all contribute to better learning that also can be well structured
and logical. And the skills and strategies are reasonably easy to learn to
use with your children. We review these in more detail in chapter 3.

KNOWING WHAT YOU KNOW
AND HOW YOU FEEL: METACOGNITION

A key aspect of thinking is awareness: awareness of what you are thinking, why you are thinking, how you are thinking, and where your thinking should be going. This awareness has been given a special name by
psychologists. It is called *metacognition*, which means *cognition about
cognition*. Research has established that the higher the levels of awareness
in early learning stages, the more effective and long lasting the learning.

Awareness allows and facilitates that the learner, the child, has more
control over the process, has more knowledge of what she is learning,
can identify mistakes and correct them, is aware of her rate of progress,
and other things that improve learning and achievement. Accompanying
what you know about what you know is the critical issue of what you

want to do, what is your child's motivation, what are his dispositions, and how can you stimulate them. Knowing is important, but wanting to know and wanting to do and wanting to achieve are even more important. Good thinking is not only a skill but also an attitude.

INTELLECTUAL STANDARDS: CRITERIA FOR THE QUALITY OF WHAT AND HOW YOU ARE THINKING

As persons operating in a complex environment, we should do everything possible to take rational command of our cognitive processes—to determine what to accept and what to reject of the information around us. Doing this requires standards for thought that guide us to consistently excellent thinking.

What are such standards? There are several, and they can be easily explained. They should be taught to our children early and also to future teachers and should be incorporated into school curricula and systematically monitored. They include clarity, accuracy, precision, logic, relevance, significance, breadth and depth, and others.

Learning and adopting the standards also includes developing positive attitudes toward clear, rational criteria and thought processes. This should be incorporated into the process of teaching your children to think. We look at this in more detail in chapter 6.

PROBLEM-SOLVING SKILLS

One long-term purpose of learning to be a competent thinker is to be able to solve problems that one confronts in life. These can be problems in a wide range of circumstances, including learning algebra, a second language, how to be a chemist or a teacher, or how to be a good parent who knows how to think and to teach his or her children to be good thinkers. This element also includes knowing how to be a good citizen, a good and discerning member of a community, a wise investor, a true professional in the work environment, and so on.

There are always many problems to solve, and we should acquire optimal skills for doing so. There are several approaches to solving problems:

- A systematic or *analytic* approach
- A *realistic* approach, stressing the problem in its context
- An *idealistic* approach, where the problem is framed on the basis of goals, values, and ideals
- A *synthetic* approach based on contrast and rapid pattern identification

- A *pragmatic* approach based on a "what works" view of problems (the trial-and-error approach)

When I explained these approaches to my father a few years ago, he said, "I would like to be able to use all of them!" We all would like to do so, but people tend to develop one or two of them as their favorite approaches, such as combining the analytic approach with the values of the idealistic approach (the most typical combination approach). Which approach one uses is often influenced by how that person learned what he or she knows over a period of years.

For example, if a child learns primarily by rote learning, by basic memorization, her problem-solving approach will tend toward the more pragmatic or realistic manners and will lack systematicity and creativity. If the child learned science and mathematics in a more dynamic and interactive way, her problem-solving approach will tend toward the analytic manner. If she grew up in a religious family, ideals and values will influence the thinking process and how she solves problems.

The five elements of good thinking—logic and structure, learning strategies, metacognition, intellectual standards, and problem solving—can be combined into a set of procedures and skills that parents can use to stimulate and facilitate improved thinking in their children. How to do this is the subject of the rest of this book.

HOW CHILDREN LEARN

Before we go on, it would be useful to talk about how children learn. The first thing to know is that children (and adults) are what we can call symbol manipulators. They learn, create, sometimes copy, and develop symbols that they use to interpret, master, and manipulate their environment. One example of these symbols is language and how rapidly children learn to master and often manipulate through language (and emotions). Think about how quickly children learn to manipulate through crying. In the newborn child, crying is a way to demonstrate some kind of discomfort, but before long, if parents are not cautious, the crying can become a way to manipulate the parents—all in the manner of symbol manipulation.

Children are born with certain innate conditions that include the internal systems for learning (perception, memory, the ability to learn languages, preferences, and even moral sense), and they build on these systems even before they are born.

From very early in their lives, children perceive what is going on around them and, bit by bit, pull information into their memories and begin, in simple ways, to organize that information. As they grow, they assimilate and organize more and more information that takes the form of mental representations that Piaget called *schemes*, little structures of information organized in some reasonable way. And so they go on, building a small repertoire in their memories of information they have accumulated from their environment and organized into little interrelated structures.

As children grow, these structures increase in number, in complexity, and in relations. For example, the group of structures we can call language grows rather quickly after about 12 months as vocabulary increases and simple grammatical constructions begin to appear. Grammar likely is innate; that is, it is an internal structural system that comes in the genes. But vocabulary is not. It is learned, and this is why talking to your children and encouraging them to answer and talk back is so vital for the development of language.

Piaget called this process the *construction of reality*, and the main points to see are that the construction comes in the form of structures (the schemas), that they are done in slightly different ways by each individual child, and that they have a reasonably predictable sequence of development. There is a relationship between biological development and cognitive or mental development. Children frame the events they see in terms of their own mental development.

Younger children have more restricted frames of reference and therefore cannot see things the same way as older children. But their learning process is basically the same. It is not (or should not be) a matter of "copying" reality but assimilating reality into a structure of transformations. Knowledge is created by the individual out of actions and out of reflections about those actions, that is, thinking. It is not simply doing things that creates or constructs knowledge; rather, it is thinking about those actions, reflecting on the doing.

Children do not learn the structures randomly, or they should not learn them that way. They are creating their own internal structures, but those should have a close relation to the world around them, to the reality in which they live. The nature of the world is that it also has multiple and overlapping structures. Learning is a combination of the construction of internal structures in a process of assuring that the internal structures have a close relationship with the external structures. There is a structure to both the child and the world around him, and in terms of schooling, there is the structure of the child and the structure of the curriculum (which represents the world around him).

In this initial learning, *action* is a key: there is a strong, even necessary, cognitive component to the concept of action. Doing things is very important for learning. And for young children (five to eight), the emphasis is on physical manipulation, which is the beginning that will lead to iconic and symbolic comprehension of relations between events and structures. In chapter 2, we examine specific learning processes in more detail.

Therefore, the overall organization of the book follows the five principles we have mentioned and will have the structure shown in figure 1.5.

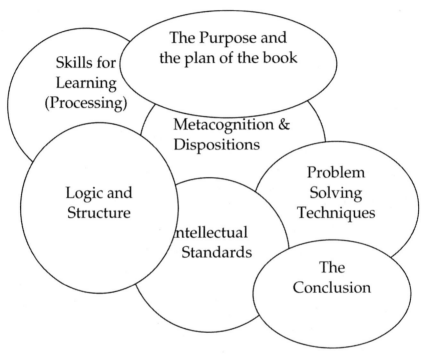

Figure 1.5.   Organization of This Book

Two

Learning and the Structure of Knowledge

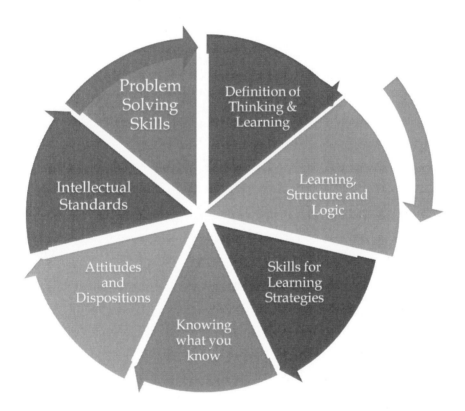

The question of how we learn and the form that our learning takes is crucial to the development of thinking. How, what, and why we learn are ideas that are interwoven. People learn through the slow *process* of accumulation of information about the world in which they live. They make associations between situations and responses. They begin to build up chunks of reasonably organized memory around which they gather more and more information, expanding what they have, expanding each "chunk," and creating new chunks.

The process of grasping the world and storing it as a representation of some form in the mind has been called assimilation and accommodation. When your child takes in new elements of information, she is absorbing or assimilating it. She is taking some experience or piece of information and finding a place for it in her existing knowledge structure. When she modifies her existing chunks so that the new information fits into some reasonable place, she is accommodating the chunks, reconfiguring the existing arrangement of knowledge so that the new information can be incorporated.

It is somewhat like rearranging blocks in a pile so that the new block fits in. Young children do not always assimilate all of the new information, sometimes only that part that they can understand. As their ability to understand grows, they accommodate more.

Sometimes assimilation and accommodation cooperate; other times, they are somewhat antagonistic. Often, the existing structure seems to be just fine, and the new information cannot find a space. Other times, the existing organization is pressured to change by the new information. When the process has worked out what has to be changed, the child (and the mental space) achieves a form of equilibrium that will be secure until the next new piece of information comes along to create a new tension.

What is it that is being accumulated; what are those "chunks" I talked about? There are several types, but the basic one is called a *scheme*, which can be either physical or mental and may be described as an action or a process used repeatedly by a child to attain goals or solve problems (thinking). A scheme is a mental structure or unit that represents some aspect of the person's world. We can think of it as a structured cluster of preconceived ideas, or as an organized pattern of thought or behavior. It could be a specific knowledge structure or cognitive representation, for example, of the self (see figure 2.1).

Another way to say this is that the scheme is a mental framework centering on a specific theme that helps children (and adults) organize social information. People use schemes to organize current knowledge and provide a framework for understanding.[1] An example would be the grasping response that infants use to investigate the physical properties of objects. The tiny child is busily investigating his surroundings, and for a time the best way he can do that is to grasp things and see their nature, weight, reaction, and so on. And he goes on developing these little schemes as he grows and increases his understanding of the world.

So as the child's learning grows, the schemes grow in size and number, and these schemata are action sequences that the child can use across a wide range of objects and situations. And the schemes become structures

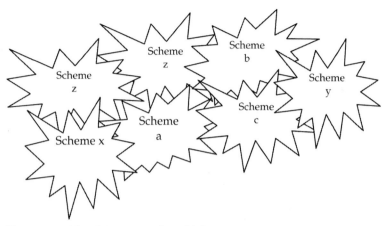

Figure 2.1. Visual Representation of Schemes

that are used to interpret and understand the surrounding world and the various topics of that world (from family to fantasy). For example, in the early school years, children construct schemes for letters, which allow them to classify an infinite variety of shapes (handwriting) into a very limited number of categories, which provide schemes for the higher-order elements when they are combined into words, which then can be combined into phrases and sentences.

Schemes in action (see figure 2.2).

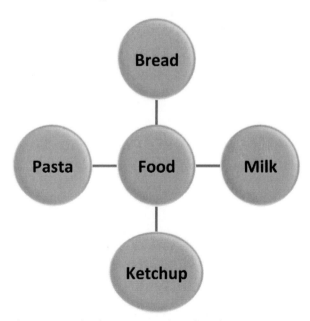

Figure 2.2. Simple Representation of a Scheme

Cognitive structures are the organized representations of previous experience; they are the mental records of what has been learned. They are relatively permanent and serve as schemes (to use Piaget's term) to actively filter, codify, categorize, and evaluate information that one receives in relation to some relevant experience. The principal idea is that while we learn, we are constantly organizing the units of what we are learning into some form of organization that we can call a *structure*.

New information generally is associated with existing information in these structures and at the same time can reorganize and restructure already existing information (this is what Piaget meant by assimilation and accommodation). These structures have been recognized by psychologists for some time. The organization of the schema, concepts, relations, and classes of information is its *structure*, which we infer from the general properties of the actions of children at a given stage of mental growth (see figure 2.3).

Skillful thinking and problem solving require types of knowledge and knowledge structures. The knowledge can be *procedural* (how to do things, such as add and subtract); *factual* knowledge, such as names, dates, numbers, and vocabulary; and *conceptual* knowledge, such as knowing the abstract and concrete concepts that make up much of the world around us.

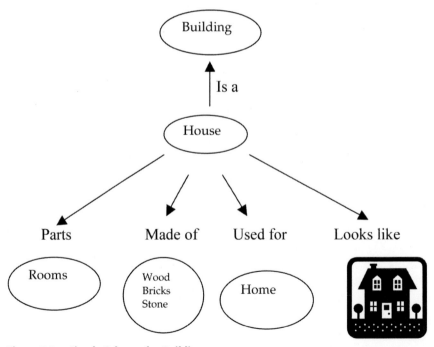

Figure 2.3.   Simple Scheme for Buildings

Concepts are a very important kind of knowledge because they facilitate learning and help solve problems. Conceptual knowledge is rich in relationships and understanding. It is a connected web of knowledge, a network in which the connecting associations are as prominent as the distinct bits of information, what we have called a structure. Conceptual knowledge cannot be learned by rote. It must be learned by thoughtful, reflective learning.

There are different kinds of concepts. First are the concrete concepts, which are things that can be seen, touched, or heard. In other words, they have some direct sensory input. Examples of concrete concepts include tables and chairs and sofas, cars and buses, horses, cows, cats and dogs, cooking, farming, and playing. The child can see them, touch them, hear them, and often smell them.

Second are abstract concepts, those that have no direct sensory input unless by metaphor or analogy. Aunt, uncle, love, hate, thought and thinking, truth, freedom, and intimacy can be thought of as abstract concepts. Imagination, friendship, freedom, and jealousy are examples of abstract concepts.

Nonverbal concepts are ones that do not always have word representations but can be understood by making mental pictures to represent their critical attributes. We see these in the following:

- The ability to recognize visual sequences and remember them
- Understanding the meaning of visual information and recognizing relationships between visual concepts
- Performing visual analogies
- Recognition of causal relationships in pictured situations

The process of painting mental pictures to aid learning and production is often referred to as visualization. Examples of nonverbal concepts include perimeter, area, volume, mass, velocity, circle, and proportion.

Nonverbal intelligence is important because it enables students to analyze and solve complex problems without relying on or being limited by language abilities. Many mathematical concepts, physics problems, computer science tasks, and science problems require strong nonverbal reasoning skills.[2]

When a student is exposed to a new concept, it is important to connect the new concept to concepts he already knows. He can do this by classifying, categorizing, recognizing patterns, and chaining. It's like finding all the "relatives" of that concept and making a family tree for the concept. For example, if a second grader is studying houses, a larger concept that houses could belong to might be dwellings, and a larger concept that dwellings could belong to might be buildings. Other buildings could be skyscrapers, hangars, and gymnasiums. All of these are buildings of some kind.

It is good to also think about what is not a house so that students will know where to "draw the line" in the larger concept of buildings. For example, caves and boxcars are not generally considered dwellings for most of us, although on occasion they are. This process of locating related concepts requires that the child do more than just memorize the concept. He must think about it and relate it to other similar concepts, thereby strengthening his basic structure.

Research shows that through this process of reflection, the child strengthens his short-term or working memory, improves his knowledge base, and increases the probability that he can recall the structure and expand it and use it for purposes such as solving problems.

A scheme (sometimes called schema) is a pattern or arrangement of knowledge that a person already has stored in his brain that helps him understand new information. For example, a student may have a definite image in his mind of what a reptile looks like by the information that he has been told about reptiles, by pictures that he has been shown, and by what he has read. When he encounters a new creature that he has never seen before but it has all of the qualities that he has stored in his brain about reptiles, he can infer or draw the conclusion that it probably is a reptile.

Some schemes are also linked to rules and predictable patterns that we have learned. For example, students can develop schemata for the tests a certain teacher gives because she always gives the same type of test. This helps a student to know how to study for the test because he knows the kinds of questions the teacher is going to ask. Schemes do not always follow a pattern or a rule, however, because there are exceptions or irregularities. For example, sometimes students have just mastered a spelling rule or a rule in grammar when the teacher throws an exception at them. In any case, using schema or patterns is a good way to make helpful predictions.

As mentioned in chapter 1, schools are not very effective in teaching how to organize schemes into structures and then reflect on them, make them stronger, and put them to use. In mathematics, for example, research suggests that children often make errors because they are blindly following procedures they have learned without having thought about them and trying to understand why and how the information could simplify the solution to important, real-world problems.

In science, students most usually memorize information about concepts like density but are not helped to see how the information can be used to interpret everyday situations. They acquire facts, not conceptual tools. School teaching should provide a framework for helping students learn to think and solve problems. Instruction that emphasizes memory for a variety of facts and definitions will appear to be effective if the teacher simply tests students about having this information.

But the information will generally remain inert and static, stored somewhere in the long-term memory, and the students will not know how to activate it for use in problem solving. Teachers should be presenting the ideas in such a way that they include the conditions under which that knowledge may be applied. But that does not happen most of the time.

Research has shown that teaching content along with information about strategies to transfer the learning affects the nature and organization of the knowledge that children acquire and increases considerably the speed with which they can become able to think effectively in a variety of rich domains. The learning of complex subject matter is most effective when it is an intentional process of constructing meaning from information and experience.

STRUCTURE: WHAT DO WE THINK ABOUT?

When we think, we think about something. That seems obvious, but it is important, and many people miss the point. "Oh, I was just thinking," but what were you thinking about? You were thinking about some form of content, idea, desire, feeling, worry, and problem; you were thinking about something, not nothing. When you are doing that, the nature of the content is important and is related to some kind of structure. When we talk about how your children are learning to think, the content about which they are thinking is a crucial issue.

The relation between the act of thinking and the stuff that one is thinking about is very important. As we have said, you cannot think about nothing. Even if you think about an empty blue sky, you are thinking about an empty blue sky. Maybe you can put a few clouds into it and maybe a sunset. But you are always thinking about something.

So the nature of that "something" is important. When we are talking about children and about how to help them become effective thinkers, the issue becomes more concrete. When they go to school and learn subjects like math, language, and basic sciences, what is it that they are learning? The answer to that question is intriguing and significant.

Knowledge has structure, which reflects the natural world. How is that structure learned in natural settings? What happens in the first three or four years before the child goes to preschool?

Much of a person's knowledge comes from direct experience with the world, which is his or her reality. Some writers say that this knowledge is generally unorganized, but that probably is not true. Children's learning is structured by their environment. Children come into the world with certain innate (biological) capabilities, and then they learn constantly from their environment for the many years. They learn to talk, eat, smile, engage with their parents and siblings, and much more.

For example, during their fourth year, we expect them to learn to throw and kick a ball, draw circles and squares, begin to copy capital letters, dress and undress, identify "same" and "different" objects, talk in short sentences so that others can understand, tell and remember parts of stories, cooperate with other children, engage in fantasy play, and understand that there are ways to solve problems. Notice that last one: by the end of the fourth year, your child should comprehend that there are ways to solve problems.

The problems may be as simple as buttoning a shirt, flushing the toilet, or finding a lost toy, but they are problems, and the child is becoming aware that they can be solved.

Individuals come across various experiences in the environment and interpret these experiences as best as they can until further experiences reinforce these interpretations or refute them. It does not usually require a teaching agent to acquire, although it could involve other teaching agents apart from a certified teacher. Examples are units of information that parents teach their children and information they pick up from the popular culture, which comes mostly through the mass media.

Both curricular knowledge and students' experiential knowledge interact in learning situations to form "knowledge of learning" that we expect students to possess in varying degrees as personal knowledge.

Another issue that is important in learning to think is the relationship between the learner (your child or children) and his or her world. Most learning comes from interaction between people, particularly between parents and their children and later between children and their teachers, but also, always, between the children and their peers and the media. Learning is influenced by social relations, interpersonal dealings, and communication with others.

As mentioned above, each person is a symbol manipulator, a being who receives information and, through various processes, manages the information. All intellectual activities, including perception, knowledge acquisition, memory, learning and using language, problem solving, imagination, and creativity, can be reduced to a few basic operations, such as encoding, storing, and retrieving information. The external world can be represented by symbols within the information-processing system (think brain). If that were not the case, we would be in big trouble. It is the case, and it is obvious but worth pointing out.

People who look at how information is processed usually take what is called a systems approach, meaning that human capacities and activities are highly interrelated. That is part of the structuralist conception of knowledge. And, logically, the human being is viewed as an active information-seeking person: he or she searches for information as part of the overall biological evolution. The person is constantly searching for useful information from the environment so as to be able to solve quotidian problems in the most effective and efficient manner.

Now add to that the idea, consistent with research results, that humans are endowed with unique innate capacities, such as the ability to use language, which is crucial for some cognitive processes.

Yet it is clear that many children in their experiences at home and in school do not put together solid structural organizations of knowledge. Often, the child's thinking is far below his potential. The most typical problems are the following:

- Thinking that is *hasty or impulsive*, without the reflection and processing it should have
- Thinking that is *narrow*, that does not include enough variety, that does not examine alternative points of view, and that does not challenge assumptions
- Thinking that is *careless, imprecise, fuzzy,* or *unrefined*
- Thinking that is *sprawling*, generally disorganized, and not goal oriented[3]

As a parent, you can help your child improve her thinking in many ways, as we begin to detail in the next chapter.

The most central insight for the appropriate teaching of thinking is that the content of thinking is nothing more or less than a *mode* of thinking, a way of figuring something out, a way of understanding something through thought:

- Historical content is a manifestation of historical thinking. When you learn, you learn not only the information involved but also the form and ways of thinking about history.
- Biological content is a manifestation of biological thinking.
- Algebraic content is a manifestation of algebraic thinking.
- Thinking about events in daily life is experiential thinking. You may think you are just thinking about your daily life, but you are also forming a way, a manner, in which to view your reality.
- Thinking about playing chess has the rules, moves, and patterns of chess as the content of thinking.
- Thinking about family has content—family members, interactions, family history, traditions, religion, and so on—all of which, by their nature, form a mode of thinking (to this day, my mother's role in our family structures how I think about families in general).

Thinking always has content. There are three ways to grasp and understand this idea. First, all "content" taught in school is substance in a subject. All subjects are areas of study. All areas of study are "things" that we are interested in "figuring out." There is no way to learn how to understand something without learning how to think about it. For example, there is no way to learn mathematical content without learning how to think about and figure out correct answers to mathematical questions and problems. That is what math is about.

Thinking involves concepts and conceptualizing. All concepts involve some form of content. There is no way to learn a body of content without learning the concepts that define and structure it. There is no way to learn a concept without learning how to use it in thinking something through. For example, to learn the concept of fair play is to learn how to figure out whether someone is being fair in the manner in which they are participating in a game.

All content is logically interdependent: things link together. Understanding one part of some content requires that we figure out its relation to other parts of that content. To learn any body of content, therefore, is to figure out (i.e., reason or think through) the connections between the parts of that content. There is (or should be) no learning of the content without this thinking process. This is a basic aspect of accommodation. The problem is that most teachers and most parents think that learning is mostly stuff to be memorized.

The majority of teachers and students currently approach content not as a mode of thinking, not as a system *for* thought, and not even as a system *of* thought but rather as a sequence of stuff to be routinely "covered" and committed to memory. When content is approached in this way, there is a very limited basis for intellectual growth; there are no deep structures of knowledge formed, no basis for long-term grasp and control, and no true thinking.

TWO SOURCES OR TYPES OF STRUCTURE

There are two types of structure: those of the field (subject, discipline, and reality) and those created by each individual child and student. The structures brought to us by reality, through the field (mathematics, science, language, and so on), are the fundamental ideas, the pervasive themes, and the basic concepts that make up the field or discipline. Learning the structure of a field is the most efficient way of learning because it helps the child see how things are related and gives him a pattern in which to place all the details otherwise forgotten. Also, it is the only way to facilitate transfer or learning (i.e., generalization).

We can show the nature of structures as related to specific subjects (math, biology, chemistry, art, and so on), but you can also think about structures in your own experience. Structures are the most important ideas, the principal components, and the pervasive themes that underlie a field or area. It might be helpful to think about your own "structures." For example, if you can play a musical instrument, you have a structure of some degree of sophistication that organizes what you know about music, about the instrument, about sounds and rhythms, about fingering, and much more.

I have two good friends who are mathematicians; they have sophisticated math structures. They can talk about, think about, and dream about math in ways I never will fully understand, although I often try. One of them also has a "farming" structure. He was raised on a small farm by his farmer father, took much interest in all the variables involved in successful farming, and learned a great deal and has it all well organized as an internal structure. He jokes that his specialty is eggplant.

Think about your own strong structures. What are they? Also, you most likely have medium structures, ones not so sophisticated but still well organized and capable of permitting you to know and do many things in terms of those structures. Think of them, jot down a few, and think of how they help you solve problems and face contingencies in your life.

Let us consider the point about the degree of development of the structures. We do not restrict the concept only to those highly advanced and well-integrated structures. Structures come in varying degrees of sophistication. My dancing structure is pathetic in spite of many years of attempts to develop it. My younger daughter's structure for Spanish is only beginning to develop since English has been her main language for about six years.

My elder daughter is a chemist. Chemistry must be the most sophisticated "structure" in a scientific field. So much information must be learned, and the process of organization (structuring—assimilating and accommodating) is crucial. Each piece interacts with each other unit, and if something is out of place, other things will not work.

Besides my psychology and education structures, which are vast, interrelated, and coordinated and allow me to exercise my profession, I have other structures that are part of my experience and certainly part of my interests. My first degree was in literature, and I have read ravenously for years, so I have a rather well-developed literature structure that allows me to choose, enjoy, evaluate, and talk about novels, genres, and authors in a reasonably refined manner.

But I also have a "cooking" structure since I learned to cook rather young and have pursued the subject over many years. The cooking structure is mostly a "doing" one (procedural), although I can also talk a bit about details of cooking, times, temperatures, what spices do, and much more. And the manifestation of the sophistication of the structure is shown by the very gourmet style of cooking I do. Both of my sisters received their initial training from my mother, just as I did. But they did not follow up to the same extent: neither can cook anywhere near as well as I can.

Again, think about your structures and those of people around you. What kind of structures does your spouse or partner have? Your mother or father? Your brothers and sisters? Your coworkers? Also, what structures would you like to see your children develop? Math, science, history, people skills, music, or physical skills (dance, sports, or drawing)? Certainly, "thinking" is a structure you desire, but, as we will see below, thinking is a structure that is infused with content, with subject matter, with stuff about which you think.

THE PURPOSE OF THINKING

And what is all of this for? What is its purpose, its *function*? In general terms, the functions are to provide solid and reliable organization to the acquired knowledge, to facilitate personal adaptation to the environment, and to provide possibilities of adapting the environment to oneself. That is, we learn so that we can better adapt to our immediate world, better respond to what is going on and what is required in our daily lives, and more easily recognize and solve problems and have a better life for ourselves, our family, and, it is hoped, the broader world; that is, with a bit of luck, we can contribute to a better world for many people.

I watch my friends, family, and students and talk to them. Sometimes, their structures are obvious, like the mathematicians and the chemists. Others are more subtle, like a few who have excellent management structures or refined personal relations and emotional structures that can be observed but are more difficult to grasp and understand.

So, we learn primarily by accumulation of concepts, ideas, information elements, and feelings that get organized into structures that help us retain the information, be able to find it more quickly when we need it, and be able to use it in some practical way to adapt to and solve problems in the world in which we live.

There are many related points in learning. The closeness of ideas (contiguity) helps to form associations that are easier to assimilate and accommodate. Developing and taking advantage of that closeness is part of learning. Giving rewards and making learning interesting are important aspects of the process. Several simple facilitators of learning are further elaborated on in later chapters. For example, motivation for learning is expanded on in chapter 5.

One of the simple but often neglected truths about knowledge is that each knowledge domain (math, science, language, history, music, and so on) has an internal structure and logic. This means that the information that composes the domain is not a random mish-mash of "stuff" but is actually an organized body of ideas that are related to each other in some logical form. The domains are sets or megastructures of well-organized and integrated compilations of information.

There are two basic ways to see that structure. One is the structure of the knowledge domain in itself: what is the nature of concrete reality? The other is the structure of how the human brain perceives and understands that knowledge structure: how do we perceive reality? For example, in the case of mathematics and physics, the external world seems to dominate in the structure of the domain, while the human brain attempts to understand and incorporate the knowledge in the domain.

In the case of history and language, there may be more interplay between the exterior and interior worlds. In language, the enormous area of idiosyncratic language (slang) demonstrates the interchange between external rules and internal invasions.

Particular types of knowledge and knowledge structures are needed for efficient learning and proficient problem solving. Much of this knowledge is conceptual in nature as opposed to operational or procedural, and powerful knowledge structures necessarily involve conceptual elements. The presence of conceptual elements in knowledge structures is the key to having a "deeper understanding" of the subject, whether it be science, math, history, language, or human relations. And, in fact, the same idea holds true in music and in many sports activities.

When we talk about the structure of a domain of learning, we are referring to the relations between elements that compose the domain.

Disciplines or domains, such as grammar, logic, mathematics, and biology, are intellectual inventions that were developed over long periods of time as a way to systematize knowledge to permit its accumulation and transmission between generations.[4]

THE CONCEPT OF THE DISCIPLINES

The disciplines, sometimes called subject matters, fields, or domains, delimit an object of study of phenomena with their own methods that define "knowledge." These methods include the following:

- The rules for identifying objects under study
- Classifying them
- Developing hypotheses
- Overall, the rules related to evidence that permit the affirmation that an observation or result is true or false

This is particularly applicable to logic, mathematics, physics, and chemistry.

During their evolution, the disciplines have developed a body of knowledge that is structured in a relatively rigorous and often hierarchical manner. The disciplines have amplified and refined their fields of study, the methods they use, and the criteria applicable to the nature of evidence. With the passage of time and the refinement of methods and techniques, there are changes in the interpretation of facts, and some of those previously considered correct, exact, or truthful can cease to be so.

Sometimes, even the nature of proof or the paradigm (model) on which they rest can be altered, such as when methods or analytic forms are too limited to be able to explain new phenomena.

Another important characteristic of a discipline is that it has a community of academic people (intellectuals and scientists) who recognize the validity of the definitions, rules, and methods of study and share the belief in the nature of the proofs required to establish scientific facts or truths and also the rules of publishing results of experiments in the discipline.

When we talk about the structure of a discipline, we refer to the organization of the knowledge as it is structured based on current scientific paradigms. In some cases, like the instrumental disciplines of grammar, rhetoric, and logic, as well as a major part of mathematics, the structures have been maintained in rather solid form over many centuries. In the case of the experimental sciences, new discoveries and new instruments and methods have led to the amplification or segmentation of fields of study with new forms of classification and order.

A few examples of organization are the following:

- The periodic table of elements.
- Algebra possesses a logical-mathematical structure.
- Mathematics has an underlying logical structure that goes from simple to complex.
- History has a chronological structure that permits comparison of events over time (diachronically or synchronically).
- Physical activities and motor skills possess a structure dictated by sequences and forms (topography) that are appropriate to them.

People become more proficient in a discipline according to how they develop internal structures that are congruent with the natural structures of the disciplines. The child codifies and stores large amounts of functional knowledge in his mind in a manner that is coherent and congruent with the nature of the discipline. This accumulation and storage allows him to identify, classify, relate, predict, and infer with greater precision and proficiency. This is what we infer when we say that someone has a head for mathematics or the sensitivity of a poet.

From the standpoint of a cognitive psychologist, there are solid reasons to favor teaching based in disciplines or in similar forms of structured organization that permit the child to resolve practical problems that involve knowledge of one or more disciplines. These problems can be presented in various forms in the school through projects, integrated curricula, or interdisciplinary activities, although they usually are not.

The disciplines continue to evolve. In the past century, we have seen an impressive increase in the number of disciplines and subdisciplines and the development of methods that are multi- or transdisciplinary. Knowledge of the disciplines is ever more important and more specialized. The dialogue between disciplines also advances as much with the intention of using the knowledge of various sciences to solve problems as in the sense of questioning the limits and appropriate forms of knowledge that the disciplines have established.

The disciplines were formed initially by Plato and Aristotle, who wished to systematize knowledge based on objective reason. The purpose of science was the search for truth, a prerequisite for their study and a noble spirit. Various curriculums (life studies plans) were developed over the subsequent centuries, including the *Trivium* (grammar, rhetoric, and logic) and the *Quadrivium* (arithmetic, geometry, music, and astronomy). These were preparatory for studying philosophy and theology. For example, the *Trivium* teaches us that language evolves from the very nature of being human.

Because we are rational, we think; because we are social, we interact with other people; and because we are corporeal, we use a physical medium. We invent symbols to express the range of practical, theoretical, and poetical experiences that make up our being and existence. Words allow us to leave a legacy of our experience to delight and educate those who follow us. Because we use language, we engage in a dialogue with both the past and the future.[5]

Essentially, this body of knowledge with distinct names is systematized as follows:

- Mastery of language
- Formal logic and mathematics
- Physical and biological sciences
- History and social sciences
- Aesthetic experience (music, art, and so on)
- Religion
- Philosophy

Closely related to the idea of the discipline is the question of how we humans can know our reality. As a part of philosophy, a subset was created and is called epistemology, or theory of knowledge, which asks the following questions:

- What is knowledge?
- How is knowledge acquired?
- What do people know?
- How do we know what we know?

There are various ways of knowing the world we live in, and these ways of knowing also lead implicitly to the disciplines. We can know the world through the following:

- Subjective validation—what we learn through our senses and our sentiments
- Objective observation—obtained through a consensus of a community of observers
- Reasoning (inductive or deductive) and logic (reflection and meditation)
- Intuition—high-speed pattern processing
- Divine revelation

Each of these five forms of knowing, combined with the seven suggested disciplines, helps us understand the notion of a discipline and how it can be managed. As parents, a little understanding of how disciplines are formed and how curricula are based on those disciplines will help you form questions and have more substantive dialogues with your children. Also, this knowledge may help you guide your children toward those areas where you think they might be most adept, have the most interest, have more talent, or other factors that might affect their aspirations.

SPECIFIC EXAMPLES

Let us start with a clear example: a map of relations about simple arithmetic. Figure 2.4 shows the basic structure of the relations between the parts of what is involved in arithmetic. We see how the four basic operations are related to each other and how they lead to somewhat higher levels, such as fractions, decimals, long division, and multiplication tables. This is a simple but illustrative example of how arithmetic subjects are related in a logical way, and the chart implicitly gives suggestions about the sequence for teaching specific aspects of mathematics.

Arithmetic

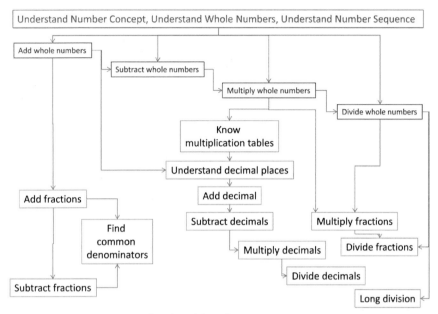

Figure 2.4. Concept Map of Basic Arithmetic

This map shows the structure of basic arithmetic and allows us to understand its parts and the relations between the parts as well as the processes used to make the parts interact to produce what they do: arithmetic.

Within arithmetic, there are many examples of simple structures (schemes) that a child learns and that can be crucial in learning more and more elaborate structures. For example, the concept of reversibility $(5 + 7 = 12, 12 - 7 = 5)$ is an obvious part of the structure of mathematics. The process of adding twos can easily be transformed into doubling, and doubling, with its inverse halving, is a powerful structural tool (schemes) for arithmetic for learning multiplication and division.

In figure 2.4, I present a simplified structure to show how concepts and functions and operations are related to each other in basic arithmetic. The chart shows the structure of arithmetic and also outlines pedagogical procedures.

Detail, unless assimilated and placed into a structured pattern, is rapidly forgotten. We can represent multiple ideas or facts in simplified ways, such as remembering a formula by which many specific facts can be derived or remembering the gist of an important soliloquy rather than remembering it word for word. Learning general or fundamental principles helps ensure that although memory loss will occur, it will not be total loss. Enough information will remain to permit the child to reconstruct the details when needed.

A good theory is the vehicle not only for understanding a phenomenon now but also for remembering it tomorrow. When students understand the fundamental principles on which factual knowledge is built, they have the ability to create and re-create the "facts" rather than being consumed with simply trying to memorize them.

Structure is crucial for understanding, learning, and thinking.

Consider a broad outline or graphic representation of the way that language is structured, as shown in figure 2.5. For speech, the primary medium of human language, there are three main components of structure: pronunciation, grammar, and meaning. Grammar is composed of morphology (the form or patterns of words) and syntax (rules for sentences). Pronunciation includes phonetics and phonology. Graphology is the study of handwriting and handwriting analysis.

Again, you probably will not spend much time on this subject in your process of teaching your children how to think. The subjects of grammar and meaning are ones that should receive a lot of attention. Syntax, vocabulary, and discourse are important issues. Morphology has to do with ways to analyze problems, something that we talk about more in chapter 7.

Let us look at a few more examples of structural representations of knowledge. The best example is the periodic table of elements, which shows the structural relations between the chemical elements of the physical world (see figure 2.6).

Chemists know that their subject has an inherent structure that is represented by the periodic table of elements, which is a reference source for learning, studying, doing research, and exchanging information

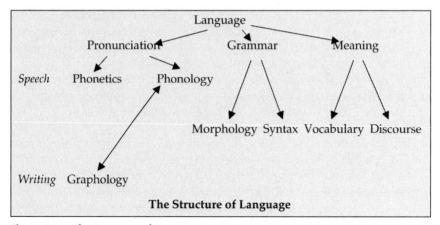

The Structure of Language

Figure 2.5. The Structure of Language

Figure 2.6. Periodic Table of Elements

hydrogen 1 **H** 1.0079																	helium 2 **He** 4.0026
lithium 3 **Li** 6.941	beryllium 4 **Be** 9.0122											boron 5 **B** 10.811	carbon 6 **C** 12.011	nitrogen 7 **N** 14.007	oxygen 8 **O** 15.999	fluorine 9 **F** 18.998	neon 10 **Ne** 20.180
sodium 11 **Na** 22.990	magnesium 12 **Mg** 24.305											aluminium 13 **Al** 26.982	silicon 14 **Si** 28.086	phosphorus 15 **P** 30.974	sulfur 16 **S** 32.065	chlorine 17 **Cl** 35.453	argon 18 **Ar** 39.948
potassium 19 **K** 39.098	calcium 20 **Ca** 40.078	scandium 21 **Sc** 44.956	titanium 22 **Ti** 47.867	vanadium 23 **V** 50.942	chromium 24 **Cr** 51.996	manganese 25 **Mn** 54.938	iron 26 **Fe** 55.845	cobalt 27 **Co** 58.933	nickel 28 **Ni** 58.693	copper 29 **Cu** 63.546	zinc 30 **Zn** 65.39	gallium 31 **Ga** 69.723	germanium 32 **Ge** 72.61	arsenic 33 **As** 74.922	selenium 34 **Se** 78.96	bromine 35 **Br** 79.904	krypton 36 **Kr** 83.80
rubidium 37 **Rb** 85.468	strontium 38 **Sr** 87.62	yttrium 39 **Y** 88.906	zirconium 40 **Zr** 91.224	niobium 41 **Nb** 92.906	molybdenum 42 **Mo** 95.94	technetium 43 **Tc** [98]	ruthenium 44 **Ru** 101.07	rhodium 45 **Rh** 102.91	palladium 46 **Pd** 106.42	silver 47 **Ag** 107.87	cadmium 48 **Cd** 112.41	indium 49 **In** 114.82	tin 50 **Sn** 118.71	antimony 51 **Sb** 121.76	tellurium 52 **Te** 127.60	iodine 53 **I** 126.90	xenon 54 **Xe** 131.29
caesium 55 **Cs** 132.91	barium 56 **Ba** 137.33	57-70 *	lutetium 71 **Lu** 174.97	hafnium 72 **Hf** 178.49	tantalum 73 **Ta** 180.95	tungsten 74 **W** 183.84	rhenium 75 **Re** 186.21	osmium 76 **Os** 190.23	iridium 77 **Ir** 192.22	platinum 78 **Pt** 195.08	gold 79 **Au** 196.97	mercury 80 **Hg** 200.59	thallium 81 **Tl** 204.38	lead 82 **Pb** 207.2	bismuth 83 **Bi** 208.98	polonium 84 **Po** [209]	astatine 85 **At** [210]	radon 86 **Rn** [222]
francium 87 **Fr** [223]	radium 88 **Ra** [226]	89-102 **	lawrencium 103 **Lr** [262]	rutherfordium 104 **Rf** [261]	dubnium 105 **Db** [262]	seaborgium 106 **Sg** [266]	bohrium 107 **Bh** [264]	hassium 108 **Hs** [269]	meitnerium 109 **Mt** [268]	ununnilium 110 **Uun** [271]	unununium 111 **Uuu** [272]	ununbium 112 **Uub** [277]		ununquadium 114 **Uuq** [289]			

*Lanthanide series

lanthanum 57 **La** 138.91	cerium 58 **Ce** 140.12	praseodymium 59 **Pr** 140.91	neodymium 60 **Nd** 144.24	promethium 61 **Pm** [145]	samarium 62 **Sm** 150.36	europium 63 **Eu** 151.96	gadolinium 64 **Gd** 157.25	terbium 65 **Tb** 158.93	dysprosium 66 **Dy** 162.50	holmium 67 **Ho** 164.93	erbium 68 **Er** 167.26	thulium 69 **Tm** 168.93	ytterbium 70 **Yb** 173.04

** Actinide series

actinium 89 **Ac** [227]	thorium 90 **Th** 232.04	protactinium 91 **Pa** 231.04	uranium 92 **U** 238.03	neptunium 93 **Np** [237]	plutonium 94 **Pu** [244]	americium 95 **Am** [243]	curium 96 **Cm** [247]	berkelium 97 **Bk** [247]	californium 98 **Cf** [251]	einsteinium 99 **Es** [252]	fermium 100 **Fm** [257]	mendelevium 101 **Md** [258]	nobelium 102 **No** [259]

between chemists and others. It has also been called the most important idea in the last millennium. What structure! You will not be teaching this to your children. That happens in 11th grade, in school, taught by a good chemistry teacher. The point is to grasp the idea that knowledge has structure.

Of course, the structure has been growing. For example, in 1800, only 27 chemical elements were known. Knowledge grows—and intriguingly so, particularly when it starts with a solid conceptual structure.

Many chemistry textbooks provide a diagram in their introductory sections showing how matter can be classified into mixtures and pure substances and then to heterogeneous and homogeneous mixtures, elements, and compounds:

Matter, the stuff from which our physical world is formed, presents to us as various types of *material*. On a first analysis, the possible phases are the following:

- Gas, such as air
- Liquid, such as water
- Solid, such as rock

In biology, the most repeated and utilized concepts are structure and functions. Plants and animals have a structure that biologists study. They also have functions that are derived from their structure. Start with a basic one (see figure 2.7).

That structure shows the relations between bacteria, the single-celled organisms called archaea, and the eucaryota, the animals we are most aware of, like plants and ourselves. Look how close we are to slime molds.

I hope it is clear that the point of this presentation is not to transform you into mathematicians, chemists, or biologists but rather to make evident that all knowledge has structure. The structure of a subject is not necessarily a mirror image of that subject in real life. Both chemistry and biology are more disordered and messy in real life than they are when represented graphically. But subjects, disciplines, ideas, and concepts do have a structure, a set of reasonably firm relations, and knowing that structure significantly improves learning.

As parents, your awareness of the underlying structure of an area will help you lead your children toward a better grasp of what they are learning. And even if you do not fully comprehend a specific structure (for me chemistry is Greek), you should appreciate the concept of structure as a fundamental for good learning and thinking.

There also is the interesting issue of kinds of knowledge and their possible integration. Certainly, we can talk of "school learning," those types of knowledge normally thought to be derived from and representing the

How animals are classified

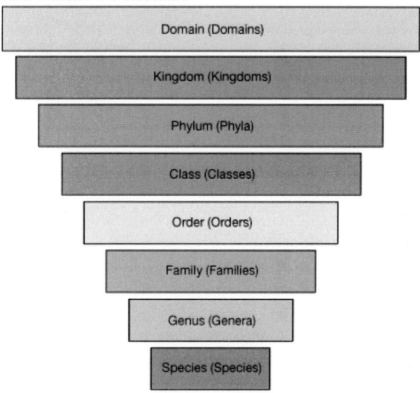

Figure 2.7. Classification of Animals

disciplines that are studied and therefore called disciplinary knowledge and also curricular knowledge.

TRANSFER OF LEARNING

An understanding of fundamental principles and ideas of a subject appears to be the main road to adequate generalization or transfer of learning. When one really understands ideas, events, or phenomena at a deep, conceptual level, that knowledge is more easily transferred to related yet different ideas, events, or phenomena. When students understand mathematical principles, they are more able to apply those principles in many different situations.

Education should focus less on "specific transfer" (applicability to tasks that are highly similar to those originally learned) and more on "nonspecific transfer," "the heart of the educational process—the continual broadening and deepening of knowledge in terms of basic and general ideas."[6] It is this type of learning that enables children to apply what they know to more remote situations, solve complex problems, and have cognitive independence. It depends not on mastery of specific skills but rather on foundational concepts and structures that can impact a wide array of problems and circumstances.

The more fundamental or basic the idea the student has learned, almost by definition, the greater will be its breadth of applicability to new problems. This is the stuff of thinking.

LEARNING: APTITUDE VERSUS EFFORT

The issue of the relation of aptitude (often thought of as intelligence or IQ) and the amount of mental effort expended in learning has been evolving. For many years, from the end of the nineteenth century until late in the twentieth, intelligence was considered a key factor in how much and how fast a child could learn. Intelligence was also thought to be a fixed factor: You had so much of it, and it would not change. During this period, most people thought that native intelligence, natural aptitudes, and talents were major explanations of success.

In the mid-1950s, a shift began that suggested that intelligence could be supplemented by more mental effort by providing children with more time to learn and more practice on the lessons they were studying. Sometimes, this was called compensatory education. There was evidence that it worked. Slower students who were given more time, more examples, and more guidance were able to achieve at the same levels of children who were more intelligent. This was a major breakthrough.

In the latter part of the twentieth century, some psychologists began to promote an even more impressive idea: Intelligence is not inflexible but can grow. How? Through sustained mental effort. Learning situations that stress a child's effort can increase intelligence. Your child can become more intelligent through continuous and concentrated effort. I suggest that while this does not mean that anyone can learn anything, it does suggest that each child can achieve much more than would be anticipated through the old-fashioned inflexible intelligence approach.

Increased mental effort can lead to improvement of student achievement and to increased intelligence. So, as parents, you will want to constantly encourage your child to apply himself, to work harder, and to do more. You will get good results. (We discuss this subject more at length in chapter 5.)

THREE

Developing Skills for Effective Learning

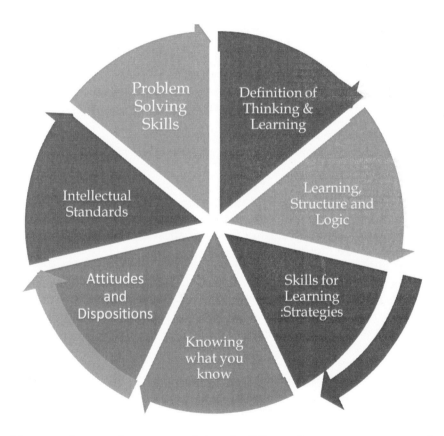

Now we know what we are doing: building schemes, structures, and megastructures with indications of how to use the information oriented generally around academic disciplines but also around life skills and activities.

And we know why we are doing this: to think better, improve our problem-solving skills, and be able to have more successful and happy lives. With this background, we start to study the five major pieces of the quality-thinking model.

The first major piece is what we call skills for learning. It is not possible to think critically and to solve problems without content (knowledge) and structure in the brain.

We can refer to the skills for learning in various ways. Frequently, they are called "learning to learn," a title that essentially is correct but not fully on target. Yes, they do have a lot to do with knowing how to learn new things—that is their major function—but the idea goes further to cover the issue of *how* a child can learn to do those things that will facilitate his or her own learning at almost any point in the process. Since learning is considered a continuous cognitive process, the approaches children acquire to help improve the process are usually called cognitive strategies.

Think about your own learning. Do you have favorite ways to learn? Do you prefer reading over listening? Do you like to underline things when you read? How do you relate what you are learning to what you already know? Is that process conscious or mostly unconscious?

TWO KINDS OF COGNITIVE PROCESSING STRATEGIES

We can divide these mental activities into three parts: initial learning skills, advanced learning skills, and skills for application and problem solving and creativity. In this chapter, we present the first two types: initial and advanced processing skills. Application and problem solving skills are discussed in chapter 7.

In learning, the first step is to do everything possible to improve learning and to make sure that what is learned is well structured, widely connected, and available for later transfer and problem solving. To do this, we require solid, reliable processes for entering new information and placing it in long-term memory such that it will be available for future use. For that, we need to go far beyond simple memorization and reach into areas of mental processing that ensure solid structure. We do that with cognitive processing strategies.

These strategies are the procedures for general mastery and control of the functioning of mental activities. They are critical in the acquisition and utilization of specific information and interact closely with the content of learning. When learning is seen from a cognitive viewpoint, we emphasize the transformations that the person makes of the stimuli he receives from his environment. This means that the cognitive terrain includes perception, attention, processing, storage (in the memory), and recovery of the information and its use in specific and direct circumstances for solving problems, in creativity, and in affective reactions.

Cognitive strategies are the management skills that a person acquires, presumably over a long period of time, to govern his or her own attention, learning, thinking, and problem-solving abilities. It is through the acquisition and refinement of these strategies that your child becomes an independent learner and thinker. It is possible to assist in the adoption of these strategies so that your child becomes a more effective learner from an early age.

The concept of cognitive strategies stresses that the child not only learns the contents of knowledge in the curriculum but also learns, subtly, about the process of learning and what he does to guide his own learning. The child learns not only *what he learns* (content and structure) but also *how he learned it*. To the degree that this learning of information goes beyond content, the student can subsequently transfer or generalize it.

The first group, initial learning skills, contains those strategies used to attend to and successfully assimilate new information (in a broad sense) into the memory. The second group contains more advanced strategies that the student uses to recover stored information; compare and contrast new and existing information; understand, use, and create metaphors and analogies; and make inferences.

INITIAL PROCESSING STRATEGIES

Processing strategies are those that your child uses, normally in an unconscious manner, to improve the possibility of acquiring and storing new information, concepts, impressions, specific data, images, general ideas, and so on. These strategies are used during attention direction (focusing) when a person orients himself and begins selective assimilation (sometimes called encoding), that is, in the selection of what he or she finds interesting.

Having filtered the stimuli, your child begins to take steps to store the memory, that is, steps to remember it. These include the efforts to recognize, reconstruct, and produce information and the child's thinking styles. The styles will affect how the child transforms the new information in order to ensure that it is remembered.

Processing is the word we use to refer to efforts to find, attend to, and enter new information impressions, ideas, and so on with the goal of storing them for a long time. We also call this *assimilation* and *accommodation*. It is clear that people learn not only through the association of their acts with the consequences but also through practice; through observation and imitation of others; through the generation of images, plans, and analogies; listening to a teacher or another person; reading; and so on, often without practice, reward, or feedback from other people.

It is also clear that various cognitive strategies facilitate such learning events.

There are two principal events or instances in these efforts: attending and the subsequent processing. First, your child has to pay attention or focus on the stimuli in some form. Then she must somehow process the stimuli for storage in the permanent memory. When we talk about processing, there are three ways to do it, corresponding to the three forms of representing things in the memory: as verbal propositions, as images, or as physical forms.

When one remembers a friend or a travel scene, it likely is stored as an image, or a "photo" of the element. When one remembers a dance move, the tango, a backhand tennis swing, or even cursive writing, what is recovered is not a verbal statement but rather a feeling of the movement, the form and the rhythm, or the topography and the sequence. When one remembers a poem, a grammatical rule, and so on, they likely remember verbal proposition, or stored phrases ("There are strange things done in the midnight sun, by the men who moil for gold."[1]).

So we process in those forms: We memorize words, we capture images, and we somehow incorporate physical sequences.

Further, there are many ways to mix these three forms to facilitate remembering by adding images to motor activities or verbal statements or vice versa.

Combining the forms somewhat complicates their explanation. But here we present the most important forms of processing and encoding (as strategies) with more emphasis on verbal propositions because they occupy such an important role in school and university learning.

These are the principal cognitive learning strategies that students use to process, encode, and remember information.[2]

I. Initial Learning Strategies
   1. Attention Strategies
   2. Physical Strategies
   3. Verbal Elaboration Strategies:
       A. Repetition
       B. Paraphrasing
       C. Asking Questions
       D. Grouping and Selective Combinations
   4. Elaboration through Objects and Images
       A. Images
       B. Episodes
       C. Mnemonics
       D. Visual Structures, Concept Maps, and Conceptual Networks
II. Advanced Learning Strategies
   1. Comparison and Contrast
   2. Use of Inferences
   3. Application or future test

INITIAL LEARNING STRATEGIES

Attention Strategies

Attention has been central to the development of the human species and the rise of sociality. It began as a way of learning social survival vigilance by paying close attention to how others perceived danger. During evolution, the ability of groups to coordinate swiftly and freely was important for survival and meant being able to share and check attention and intention in the pursuit of goals. Evolutionary pressure on paying attention to others was enormous. The ability to pay attention to relevant stimuli is very important.

Children do not learn adequately if they are not looking at and listening to the important aspects of what they are to learn. Attention strategies serve to help one learn how to observe the environment, how to develop the capability of perception from the sense organs, and how to orient oneself toward material—how to perceive and select the most important aspects of the learning situation.

There are a few basic attention strategies. The first is search or vigilance. This means the efforts to find one or more items in a perceptual field that may be either rich or poor in stimuli. Much of the learning activity of school students requires that they actively search for relevant and useful stimuli. It is a bit like "Where's Waldo." Word search puzzles are typically available in the morning newspapers. Also, books of puzzles can be found at newsstands, and there are several sites on the Internet that offer puzzles.

These puzzles do help children learn to pay close attention to visual stimuli (letters) and figure out which combinations make words.

The second form of attention strategies is the management of divided attention (also called distraction), a condition that requires that the student captures stimuli from two or more sources. The simplest form is when the student is trying to listen to the teacher while also making notes. In terms of attention, this form is difficult because the child must alternate channels of attention between listening and writing. Think about what happens when you are talking on the phone and another person comes up and begins talking to you.

The excess of information makes concentration difficult. Because of cognitive load, the person tends to pay attention to one source of information at a time and when paying attention to two sources will alternate quickly back and forth between the sources. The tendency to get distracted is an indicator of the difference between good students and poor students: The better students can better grasp inputs from two sources with less distraction.

The third form of attention is the most important—sustained attention—which is sometimes called concentration. It is the ability to focus one's efforts on one situation (event, stimulus, and issue) for a relatively long period without being distracted by extraneous stimuli. Concentration is related to persistence, as we will see in chapter 5. Strategies for increasing sustained attention normally involve metacognition.

Physical Strategies

Students often have to learn many physical movements, called motor skills, as part of their education. Handwriting is a complex physical skill, for example. Formulating words in one's native language and particularly in a foreign language requires physical skills. Graphic art, drawing, and coloring are all physical activities. Learning to type or to play a musical instrument involves physical activities. All the sports one learns involve physical activities.

For the most part, the development of physical skills is taught through demonstration and extensive practice. In handwriting, children draw the letters bit by bit and receive prompting from their parents and their teachers as to the adequacy of their efforts. They continue to practice for long periods of time.

While practice is important, it also is possible to speed up learning by the application of some strategic efforts through which the practice may be refined. For example, mental imaging of the motor effort has been seen as one way to improve performance. The basketball player who imagines himself successfully making a free throw by mentally "seeing" the steps and actions he will take is more likely to make the free throw.

The basic situation with motor skills is the need to polish the topography (form) of the response and refine and ensure that the sequence is optimal. Normally, this is done through extensive practice. Physical movements require time and repetition to be refined. Through mental

RED AND ROVER ©2011 Brian Basset.

imagery, it is possible to refine the topography and the sequence and develop guidelines for implementation by creating images in the mind that are examples of optimal form and sequence.

Parents can help their children pay attention to the sequence of motor skills by guiding them, for example, through the strokes involved in writing letters or in tracing and drawing. Parents should ensure that the child is following form and sequence and also repeating the acts several times. There is no way around the importance of practice.

Verbal Elaboration Strategies

This is a very broad category, as you can imagine. By verbal elaboration, we mean the major strategies a child uses to learn new things that involve mostly words. This is what the child does to actively work with the material that comes in the form of verbal propositions (sentences), asking and answering questions about the material, describing and generating relations with things he already knows, figuring out implications, and much more. In general school learning, words, phrases, associations, sentences, and derivation of meaning are major portions of what must be mastered.

Verbal elaboration can be involved in four basic activities when learning: listening, speaking, reading, and writing. Given the nature of school learning with its emphasis on the accumulation of facts, rules, and procedures, much of what your child learns comes from listening and writing. The most frequent activity in the classroom is that the teacher is talking and the students are listening. But it is also important to develop children's capacities to express themselves, and as parents you play a major role in that development.

Here I present the most typical verbal learning strategies.

REPETITION

The first major strategy, one that most likely is inborn, is repetition.

When someone gives you a phone number and you do not have a pencil at hand, what do you do? You repeat the number until it "locks in" or until you can find a pencil.

This strategy is basic and simple and attempts to record the information one is receiving. It is so prevalent that it is called "memorizing," which is an incorrect term because anything a child does to process information is memorizing. This strategy is simply repeating what has been heard or seen in the working memory until at some point it gets recorded in long-term memory. It is often referred to as rote learning.

Repeating is the most widely used form of learning in school. It is most often seen in cases where precision is important, such as multiplication tables, chemical formulas, events and dates in history, names of authors, and so on.

As a learning strategy, we recognize that it is easy to acquire. In fact, it may be a scheme that exists innately in our system. Therefore, it would appear that its use requires no special training. To improve its use, many children are taught strategies that are mental exercises that build concentration and memory span through so-called brain games, of which there are many, all available on the Internet.[3] Memory training can be useful, but I am not an enthusiast of these measures, preferring other elaboration strategies that are explained later in this chapter.

What is important to point out is that as a learning strategy, repetition is *not* very effective. Memorized information that presumably goes into long-term memory often does not go in, and, if it does, usually about half of it disappears within the first 48 hours. Also, if your child has learned a chain of information, such as a poem or other verbal chain, if one small aspect of it is forgotten, the whole chain tends to get lost or completely confused.

The best way to improve the effectiveness of memorization is to modify the strategy and move toward higher forms of verbal processing, particularly verbal elaboration, visual elaboration, comparison, inferences, and so on.

Paraphrasing

When one takes an idea and transforms it into her own words, she is paraphrasing. This means a restatement of a text, passage, or group of ideas into another form or other words that clarify the meaning and make it easier for the child to assimilate and accommodate. The restatement of texts into other words is an effective studying or teaching strategy under the right circumstances. It is done in order for the learner to transform the vocabulary into words with which he is more comfortable or to take passages that present important points, explanations, or arguments but that don't contain memorable or straightforward wording.

The child accommodates the information in words she knows that are more natural, meaningful, and comfortable and that relate to her existing schemes and therefore fit better into existing structures. Further, while doing the paraphrasing, the child is investing more mental effort into the learning situation, thereby increasing the probability of successful memorization. This strategy may include reinterpretation, combination with existing known information, some kind of amplification or extension, and an improvement in familiarity.

Paraphrasing is useful in many subjects, such as history, social studies, literature, and others. It is not appropriate when precise meaning is required. You cannot, for example, paraphrase the multiplication table, nor would you go to a pharmacist who is paraphrasing chemical formulas.

Parents should stimulate the practice of paraphrasing whenever it is appropriate. For example, when reading stories, you can ask your child to restate events in his own words, and you can ascertain if he really comprehends the story:

You can prompt:
- Can you explain that in your own words?

You can model the concept:
- The way I would say that is . . .
- Your grandmother used to say . . .
- How would this same idea sound if we used easier words?

As your child paraphrases, you must provide quality control and feedback. It will be easy, particularly at first, for your child to get off the track, mix up the concepts, and so on. You must correct and guide with simple questions that will help her get it right:

- Are you sure you have stuck to the key ideas?
- Did you get off track in your restatement?

ASKING QUESTIONS

> "We're too concentrated on having our children learn the answers," he summarizes.
> "I would teach them how to ask questions—because that's how you learn."
>
> —Historian David McCullough

Another apparently innate learning process is the asking of questions. By asking questions, the learning process goes much deeper. The strategy is very powerful if used correctly. Children naturally ask questions, and if their parents learn how to respond well to the questions and learn how to ask questions of their children, many positive things happen.

Someone has suggested that, on an average, children ask as many as 300,000 questions by the time they become five years in age. That is an exaggeration because it would mean about 200 questions per day from the time they learned to talk. But certainly, they do ask a lot of questions. How parents respond to these questions will influence the way their children can develop in their thinking in later life. The most important tip is to get actively involved with them to answer their questions and provide appropriate solutions.

The basic aspect of curiosity is to look at things in your children's way and in the right manner.

The school likely will not develop skills and habits in asking and answering questions. Several studies have found that two-thirds to four-fifths of the questions teachers ask in school require only factual answers, usually direct recall of material in textbooks. About 15 percent of questions are procedural. Less than 20 percent of questions actually require students to think, and even then, the thinking is at a rather low level.

Often, teachers ask a question and expect an immediate answer. Rarely do teachers wait for 10 or more seconds so that their students can think about and formulate an answer to the questions. Further, teachers do not model the question-and-answer routine, nor do they openly encourage students to ask questions. One study found that less than one question per class was student initiated.

There are several advantages to systematically using and developing questioning behavior.

First, children learn more and often better (in the sense of more mental effort) and develop better linkage to existing schemes and structures. Question answering and question generation is a good means of ensuring active mental processing, central focusing, and other comprehension-fostering and -monitoring activities.

Second, children learn that asking questions is a logical way to approach the unknowns in life, to find out many things that would not have arrived without asking about them. (One thing that is very damaging to children is to grow up in an environment where questions are not to be asked or do not get answered.)

Third, the process of asking, when received by parents or teachers with a certain degree of enthusiasm, is a major step toward stimulating the child's general sense of curiosity, a vital tool in growth, self-efficacy, and survival. Major studies show that children significantly improve their learning when they are involved in answering and creating questions.

There are many variations on how to ask and answer questions. The first thing a parent should think about is the purpose of the question: Why are you asking it? There are four general levels of responses that you will be looking for.

First is recall of basic facts, remembering the little pieces of a scheme, like who was the first president. This is an important category. One good way to approach questioning is to start at this level and then move on to more complex levels. The presumption is that if your child does not know the basic facts, she will not be able to answer more complex questions.

At this level, you are looking for questions to ensure that your child has grasped the basic points. What, when, how, where, and who are the beginning points. The "why" question gets somewhat more serious. Parents should pay close attention to their children's questions from early on, as soon as they can string together three or more words.

In a direct and simple form, the parent can raise questions directly related to the immediate environment:

- What or who is that?
- How does it work?
- What does it do?
- How many are there?
- When did it happen?
- When you did that, what happened?

These questions direct attention, focus it on specific issues, and increase the possibility that your child will retain specific and related information. Good basic questioning significantly helps strengthen the underlying structure and schemes where the information is stored. The questions help children review existing schemes, assimilate and reorganize them, and broaden the underlying structure.

Questions and Reading Comprehension. Using questions is good when trying to teach reading comprehension to your child. The ability to read and fully understand what has been read and then to be able to explain it is one of the most important elements of mastery required to be a successful learner. One of the basic tasks is to develop the ability to recognize and decode words automatically (i.e., without having to pay attention to the decoding steps).

When decoding is automatic, the reader will be able to read at a faster rate, say, 45 words per minute, which will allow your child to focus on sentence integration and semantic processing. If your child reads too slowly, the information being read will tend to fade from the working memory before sentence or paragraph completion, thereby impeding comprehension.

The child's ability to read is one of the highest predictors of his future success in school. Questioning is a good way to guide attention and strengthen comprehension.

To the questions listed above, we may add the following:

- What does this word mean?
- What does this sentence mean?
- What is the most important sentence in this paragraph?

- Who is the principal person or character in this story? Who are the secondary characters?
- What is happening in the story?
- Does the principal character initiate action?
- What does the character want to achieve; that is, what is his goal?
- Where does the story take place (setting)?
- Is someone going from one place to another?
- What is the basic point or purpose of the story?

The second level is one where your child should be able to describe situations, clarify information, use maps, demonstrate rules, and show knowledge of order and evidence of comprehension.

Questions may include the following:

- What are the key vocabulary words? Do you know what they mean?
- What is the main idea of this paragraph, article, or chapter?
- Can you summarize the paragraph?
- How are ——— and ——— alike or different?
- What is the funniest/scariest/best part of the story?
- What is the author (or the article or story) trying to convince us of?
- What are the strengths and weaknesses of ———?
- How is this idea related to that idea or concept?
- Give me a new example of ———.
- How does the author put the ideas in order?

The third level is the one where some kind of analytic thinking is required, that is, logical reasoning, explanation, and identification of principles and concepts:

- Are any of the main characters like you or like somebody you know? What makes you think so?
- Why do spiders weave webs?
- What happens when water boils?
- Why does rain fall?
- What would happen if ——— and ——— are combined?
- What is the difference between … and …?
- How could ——— be used to ———?
- What are the strengths and weaknesses of ———?
- What do you think would happen if we had no bones?
- How are bones and muscles similar? Different?

The fourth level is when you expect your child to be able to demonstrate evaluative thinking, showing criteria for determining the adequacy, appropriateness, or quality of ideas, concepts, and principles:

- What conclusions can you draw from this?
- Why is it important that ———?
- How does the main idea of this paragraph, article, chapter relate to what you already know about the topic?
- Can you identify the three most important ideas that can be related to the main idea?
- Do you think that character A had her feelings hurt by what character B said?
- Was what character B did right or wrong?
- Would any of your friends/family enjoy this book? Why or why not?
- Could you come up with another good title for this book? What would it be?
- If you could change the ending of this book, what would it be?
- Do you think this book would make a good movie? Why or why not?

There are also prompting questions that may be used at any level. They are designed to get your child to amplify his responses:

- Can you tell me a little more?
- Do you agree with me on this subject?
- What would you like to know about this story (about dinosaurs, space travel, and so on)?
- What do you think we should do next to solve this problem?
- What is your opinion about these drawings/pictures?

If we amplify the questions a little—"Why?," "When?," "What for?," "What does that mean?," "How do you know?"—the questions begin to foment relations between schemes and within existing structures and help develop internal connections and increase the meaningfulness of the information.

Look at the issue of who asks the questions and when. In general terms, questions that are asked prior to presenting new information have the tendency to facilitate the learning of facts in a verbatim form, while questions that are asked after new information has been presented seem to strengthen conceptual learning or learning of nonspecific information.

Questions that are asked before reading a selection to your child orient attention toward the search for specific information while questions asked after reading the story call attention to general opinions about it.

In the cognitive strategy of asking questions, we have a group of general issues. For example, specific questions are better than general ones. That is not always easy for parents because they sometimes do not know the specifics of the curriculum that is being taught. But if your child brings a homework assignment, then the specifics are stated in it.

Another issue is the development of the ability to provide data to justify or defend a response given to a question. In a reading task, when asked to interpret the meaning of a section, can your child indicate the specifics in the story that would justify his or her conclusions? Is the response plausible and believable? Is the response relevant to and directed toward the questions that were asked?

Teaching children to generate their own questions cannot be overemphasized. It is a significant contributor to helping your children become more curious, reflexive, and inquisitive. Generally, the act of asking questions, which is modeling the concept, should lead to your child's ability to ask questions. You will want to encourage her to ask questions, and you may need to prompt her to do so:

- What questions would you ask about this reading?
- What do you think you should ask about that?
- Can you suggest the most important aspect of this subject?
- If you were to ask a classmate about this, what would be the key question?
- When you are thinking about this, what do you ask yourself about it?

One small risk when asking questions is overprompting, that is, providing too much information to the child so that finding the answer does not require any significant effort. The question should give enough information so that she can search in her memory for the answer but not give so much information that she can easily find the answer. That would lead to problems of attribution (see chapter 5).

Then you must think about redirection, that is, turning the tables a little. I always say that the only answer to a question a child asks is "What do you think?" If you answer the question, you may be depriving your child of the opportunity of thinking more about it. Gently returning the question can stimulate your child to dig a little deeper.

GROUPING AND SELECTIVE COMBINATIONS

In selective grouping, also called chunking, information is reorganized into smaller sets so that the working memory can handle it better. This is done by finding logical characteristics that allow for chunking. Remember that I have stressed the importance of the structure of what is being learned. Grouping is one step in the process of creating and understanding structure.

There are simple forms of chunking or grouping to facilitate memory processing by bringing words or letters or ideas into relations that help to remember them.

In initial reading, chunking means to break words into parts so that your child can learn the parts and then combine them to have full words. Examples are the following:

- Sat has one chunk: *sat*
- Feather has two chunks: *fea ther* or *feath er*
- Artifact has three chunks: *ar ti fact* or *art i fact*
- January has four chunks: *Jan u ar y* or *Jan u a ry*

When teaching reading and spelling, breaking the words into chunks facilitates understanding of how words are made up of syllables and how the syllable chunks can be memorized and then used in various settings. Reducing strain on short-term memory will facilitate assimilation and accommodation and prepare a schema about how to divide and recombine words.

Take, for example, *pre-*, which is the first part of *prefix*. It is also the first chunk of *prepare, preflight, predict, pre-affect, pre-assign, pre-distrust, precision, precise, predator, predicate*, and so on. My *Webster's Unabridged Dictionary*[4] provides more than 1,500 possibilities. Learning to chunk can truly help develop vocabulary. Look, for example, at the role of prefixes (see table 3.1).

Table 3.1.

Prefix	Meaning	Example, Key Word
anti-	against	antifreeze
de-	opposite	defrost, deduce, demean
dis- *	not, opposite of	disagree
en- em-	cause to	encode, embrace
fore-	before	forecast
in- im-	in	infield, implant
in- im- il- ir- *	not	injustice, impossible, irrational
inter-	between	interact
mid-	middle	midway
mis-	wrongly	misfire, misplace
non-	not	nonsense
over-	over	overlook, overcome
pre-	before	prefix
re- *	again	return
semi-	half	semicircle
sub-	under	submarine, subsume
super-	above	superstar
trans-	across	transport
un- *	not	unfriendly
under-	under	undersea

* These four are the most frequent prefixes, accounting for 97 percent of prefixed words in printed English.

Chunking information, or combining small bits together in short-term memory, is another strategy that students can use to increase their memory capacity. The usefulness of chunking depends on how much knowledge a child already has. The more knowledge your child has on a topic, the more likely he or she can "chunk" incoming information into larger and more meaningful units. This is why knowledge itself adds to one's ability to solve complex problems. Children who use chunking are more likely to be strategic about their learning. Parents can help their children become more strategic by explicitly teaching them strategies like chunking.

The following digits can be seen as a random list of numbers: 19411812. As we have insisted, random or meaningless information strains the limited capacity of short-term memory. If your child "chunks" the information into two dates (1941: United States entered World War II and 1812: the year of the last War of Independence from England), it leaves more space in short-term memory, which can be used for more information or for processing existing information. Chunking allows several units of information to be compressed into a single meaningful unit or chunk.

The most important aspect of the chunking idea is that it must be done conscientiously. The child must look at the information and ask himself how it can be organized to make it easier to understand, grasp, and remember. This means more effort, more accommodation, and the development of a better internal structure of the information.

One of the most notable forms of grouping is the construction of conceptual networks and other interconnections of concepts and ideas in a manner that is effective for organizing and processing new information. The idea is to consciously develop the relations of propositions, phrases, concepts, and sets of concepts into networks. One of the main suggestions of cognitive psychology is that the individual naturally tends to structure the information she receives from the world in which she lives.

The closer the internally developed structures reflect objective reality, the stronger and more useful they will be. The networks can be used in learning propositional information (descriptive, as in the social sciences), abstract concepts, and information about processes and procedures (like the rules of spelling).

These networks can be constructed in diverse forms and for almost any relation between events or concepts. One form is hierarchical construction. Another form is the development of the networks by searching for the types of relations that may exist between the parts of the information that the child is studying. For example, the relation "part" exists when the content of the lower element of the object, process, idea, or concept is contained in the higher element (see figure 3.1).

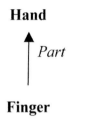

Hand

Part

Finger

Vehicle (Car, Truck, etc.)

Part

Wheels

Figure 3.1. Part/Whole Examples

When the content of the element is a member or example of a class or category of processes, ideas, concepts, or objects contained in a higher element, the relation is an "example" (see figure 3.2).

Dimension is another example of relations. The basic idea is large versus small (see figure 3.3).

Relations also have multiple connections, as in the definition of the triangle, which can be represented as shown in figure 3.4.

In this case, the layout creates four triangles, so the child will remember the four elements that compose the definition of the triangle. (This layout also is an image, discussed later in this chapter.)

The relations in a "chain" imply cause and effect of some type when the object, idea, process, or concept is an element that carries or results in an object, idea, process, or concept in the other element. Cause and effect is the relationship between two things when one thing makes something else happen. If we eat too much food and do not exercise, we gain weight. Eating food without sufficient exercise is the "cause"; weight gain is the "effect." There is research that suggests that children begin to recognize cause-and-effect relations in their environment as early as at 27 months.

Understanding the relationship between causes and effects helps your child learn how the world works. Children's natural curiosity about the world often involves cause and effect without their realizing it. If they grasp cause-and-effect ideas, they will be able to make predictions when they read either fiction or nonfiction. This helps with their comprehension. History is full of cause-and-effect relationships. Science concepts are also full of these relations, such as that heating water causes it to boil. Children can better predict the outcome of an experiment if they understand causal relationships:

Heat >> causes >> water to boil

It is then easy to generalize to other effects from fire, hot stoves, and so on:

Heat (burn) >> causes >> pain

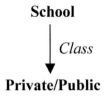

School

Class

Private/Public

Dogs

Class

Poodle, Terrier, Lhasa Apso, Dachshund

Figure 3.2.   Member of Class Examples

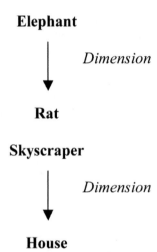

Elephant

Dimension

Rat

Skyscraper

Dimension

House

Figure 3.3.   Large vs. Small Examples

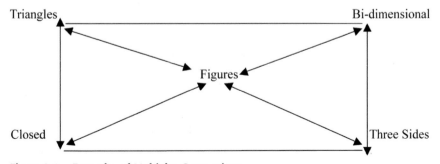

Triangles

Bi-dimensional

Figures

Closed

Three Sides

Figure 3.4.   Examples of Multiples Connections

Here is a more sophisticated example, one that your child will recognize if she has the correct background information:

*Direction of wind shifts >> the antelopes
smell the lion >> the antelopes run to escape*

You will want to teach your child to know and notice the words that signal cause-and-effect relations, such as the following:

- *because, so, so that, if . . . then*
- *consequently, thus, since, for, for this reason*
- *as a result of, therefore, due to, this is how*
- *nevertheless, and accordingly*

In addition, your child should learn different kinds of relations, such as cause-and-effect relationships where the relationship is stated clearly, for example, that heating water will cause it to boil. She should also learn to identify reciprocal cause-and-effect relationships: effects that may be part of a chain where one effect goes on to cause a second effect, which may then cause a third effect, and so on.

The evidence of the effectiveness of this type of strategy is notable. One researcher taught fourth graders to generate verbal and spatial relations and found significant differences in learning when compared to a control group who did not learn how to generate the relations. When taught how to prepare a summary sentence for each paragraph of a reading assignment, sixth-grade students had reading comprehension scores that were twice as high as the control group.

Let's briefly consider note taking, which is part of all learning strategies but is particularly useful in verbal elaboration strategies. Note taking is a strategy that parents can use to support student learning. Without explicit instruction in note taking, however, many students simply write down words or phrases word for word without analysis (or good effect). Good note takers summarize what they are reading (or hearing) to arrive at a section of meaning that they are much more likely to retain.

Children also benefit from using their notes as an organizer of their learning. You can prompt your child to review and refine her notes, particularly when it is time to prepare for an exam, write a research paper, or use some other summative assessment of learning. Further, as we now move on to the use of images, visual structures, concept maps, and comparison and contrast, you will realize that all of these strategies involve note taking, normally at a higher thinking level.

In the following section, we look at the continuum of complexity of cognitive strategies for learning. We confront the intriguing sequence of moving from the use of simple images to abstract images to learning comparison and contrast to using analogies, metaphors, and similes and then to understanding and using inference. I hope you will be able to appreciate the links between these strategies and how each contributes to the following until we have a solid picture of how to improve learning.

Elaboration through Objects and Images

The use of objects in initial learning, particularly of basic mathematics concepts, can be a valuable source of support but also has limitations. Using objects such as blocks, balls, tiles, popsicle sticks, marbles, checkers, and related objects to teach counting and number sense and basic operations such as simple addition and subtraction is useful in the very early stages of learning (between ages four and six) but loses power as children grow older. The child from five years on can grasp symbolic concepts (+, −, /, *, and =) with reasonable ease.

Research has shown that use of manipulable objects tends to reduce the possibility of transferring knowledge to other written and symbolic forms of representation. The basic idea is to use objects with your child when she is young to develop number sense, counting, and simple operations but to move into more symbolic representations, as these will give greater help to transferring basic learning to higher levels of achievement.

One major way to store information in the memory is through the use of visual images, a form that preserves as continuous dimensions some of the physical attributes of what is being remembered. Think about our senses. We can say that the primary sense is sight: We see the world around us, and that input is very important. So it is logical to think that images—sort of like photographs of what is going on—are a primary source of our memory about what is happening or what has happened and contribute to the development of the structure of the mind.

IMAGES

Without image, thinking is impossible.

—Aristotle

The use of images can facilitate learning because often clarity and meaning are facilitated when ideas, concepts, and information are transformed into visual images and objects. Visualization is a framework for learning. The process of alteration and adaptation organizes ideas in ways that make them more accessible, concrete, and understandable (in diagrams or maps) or allows information to be seen differently, in a more meaningful and personal way, and helps produce new insights and learning.

When we use images, the goal is to change and improve the way we see and interpret things, leading to new organization and understanding that create new knowledge and reaffirm the structure of learning.

We live in a highly visual world not only because sight is such an important sense but also because visual imagery plays a dominant role in shaping our contemporary world. Think about television, cinema, video games, and DVDs—pictures and images that represent, mediate, and make parts of life comprehensible. Visual symbols provide a concrete base for the abstract use of symbols through activities of observation followed by abstract representations that facilitate reconceptualization and understanding of experience before describing it verbally.

Since pictures and illustrations are analogues of experience, they may be able to capture and communicate concrete experience in various ways.

Multiple-media awareness and knowledge are necessary to meet the challenges of modern knowledge-based society. These include being literate in written words; understanding the organization, forms, and systems of meaning of visual messages; having knowledge of how to use computers; and understanding that different cultures have different approaches to a wide range of issues. Visual literacy is visual thinking, the ability to turn information of all types into pictures, graphics, and other forms to help comprehend and communicate the information. It involves learning to interpret and to create visual messages.

The presence of visual elements in school lessons is increasing through the integration of images and visual presentations in textbooks, manuals, classroom presentations, and computer interfaces. Textbooks often have many pictures, and too many of these are more distracting than helpful in learning.

The first form for using images is the simple association with information (data, concepts, and ideas) to be represented. If I ask you how many windows are on the front side of your house or apartment, you will recover from your mind an image of your house and count the windows. How long it will take you to answer will depend on how many windows your house has. If I ask you to remember a seaside resort, the face of a known person (like your mother), the panorama of a famous hotel, the latest Jaguar XF sedan, you will most likely recover an image.

Many objects and spatial relations that are in the image can be stimulated and managed in order to improve learning, and the effect of using such relations then becomes a cognitive strategy. The use of words that stimulate images or instructions from the teacher or parent to the child in the sense of teaching him how to generate his own personal images will certainly facilitate learning.

Prior to eight or nine years old, the child may not have enough experience to generate his own images, so the help of a parent or teacher can be important. After this age, the child can generate images, and their use in improving learning has been amply demonstrated in experiments and in natural classroom settings[5] (see figure 3.5).

An initial level of using images is for exploration. Your child probably enjoys using images to study dinosaurs, the leaves on trees, or the patterns of the clouds. This study of patterns will be useful later in learning the alphabet and numbers.

A well-known example of using images in learning is the pairing of letters of the alphabet with pictures to help your child remember. Through these pairings, your child learns the letters by associating them with the image of a known object: *A goes with Apple*. This helps develop a support for the letter.

You can imagine myriad examples. Figure 3.6 provides a chart to help children identify tools.[6]

And children seem to love dinosaur pictures[7] (see figure 3.7).

Another form of using images is to photograph experiences in order to re-create them later. Your child can then use the images from a vacation trip to re-create a sequence of events such as "First we saw the lions, then the hippopotamus, and then we got on a truck and drove to where we could feed the giraffes."

Figure 3.5. Letter/Image Associations

Figure 3.6. Image and Tool Name Associations

Figure 3.7. Dinosaurs

It should be clear that images also can be used to motivate your child.

To improve effectiveness even more, your child should learn to go beyond simple associations as memory aids and use images as links or mediators between a stimulus and a response or between two elements that she wishes to link together and remember.

EPISODES

Episodes are memories of events that occur with a certain sequence and in a certain place or moment in the personal history of the child. Episodes are "stories," or "scripts," normally composed of images (although they sometimes include feelings, sounds, and smells). When a student remembers how to go about a chemical procedure, he has stored the sequence in his memory as a group of images in a sequence.

If you remember the first time you went to a football game, a dance, a ballet presentation, you are probably remembering a series of events you have stored as images. The same thing is true of movies. If your child remembers *Ice Age 1*, she is remembering a series of images organized as episodes that together make up the movie.

How we understand episodes has been studied less than our understanding of objects or physical events. As children mature from infancy to adolescence, they advance from simple perception to deeper inference, from basic description to explanation, from uncomplicated identification to temporality to causality and to goals, and from isolated events to whole episodes and then to links between episodes.

To understand longer sequences of events, we need considerable memory resources. We can distinguish between semantic and episodic memory. Semantic memory stores general knowledge, such as my knowledge of words, concepts, and ideas. Episodic memory records are particular events that are remembered as they were experienced and can be more or less located in time and a specific place.

For example, I can remember the last time I was in an automobile accident, which was more than 15 years ago, and I can immediately see the street corner and remember looking in the mirror to see that the guy behind me was coming too fast and my yelling at my wife to hold on. But I cannot remember the first time I kissed a girl because that was when I was four years old, a long time ago. We know that our episodic memories are not extraordinarily accurate or exact but are only partially constructed. We tend to remember deep rather than superficial details, the essence rather than the specifics.

There are several ways to use episodes to teach. The first and simplest is to sit with your child while she watches *Sesame Street* or *The Little Einsteins* and ask questions and direct attention about the contents and settings of the episodes. There is much research evidence to show that this simple interaction increases learning.

A second method is to ask your child to recall episodes from her favorite television programs or movies and lead and guide recall with questions such as the following:

- How did it start?
- Who was involved?
- What happened next?
- What was the problem?
- How did it end?

A third method is to ask questions while sitting with your child watching movies or television series. If you are watching a rerun or DVD of *Ice Age*, *Shrek*, or *Tangled* or something on the Discovery Channel or the National Geographic Channel, you could sit with your child and pepper him with questions related to the sequence and critical events of the movies. This will build a much stronger schema and structure for understanding episodes and episodic grammar.

Also remember that animations such as *Mickey Mouse*, *Roadrunner*, and *Bugs Bunny* are all forms of episodes about which you can ask your child questions.

Doing this strengthens your child's memory in general and in relation to episodic information in particular. It also helps create sensitivity to and cognitive strategies for deriving information from episodes and retaining and using the information for other learning events, including writing stories and learning how to do chemistry experiments.

A fourth method is to re-create previous events as episodes. For example, if your child is studying early American history, you can re-create the midnight ride of Paul Revere. You could do this in the house or in the yard.

You could designate one place as Charlestown, where Revere received the news that the British were coming by sea. Then you could designate another place (a room?) as Medford, toward which Revere rode. Then you could designate another place as Lexington, where Revere gave his message to John Adams and John Hancock, waking up residents as he traveled; then on to Concord, where he was briefly held by the British; and, finally, back to Lexington, where he saw part of the Battle of Lexington Green. If you can get other members of the family or school peers involved, it can be great fun and a significant learning event.

MNEMONICS

When a person constructs a special relation between aspects of a stimulus in terms of special associations, he is using a mnemonic (named for

Mnemosyne, the Greek goddess of memory). A mnemonic is a technique for remembering something.

"*I* before *e* except after *c* or when sounded as *a* in neighbor or weigh" is a spelling mnemonic. A mnemonic for remembering the number of days in each month is the following:

Thirty days hath September, April, June, and November,
All the rest have thirty-one, except for February, alone,
Which hath but twenty-eight, in fine,
Till leap year gives it twenty-nine.

I learned this when I was rather young and still use it when necessary.

One way to create mnemonics is through the use of the first letter of key words. For example, how do I remember the spelling of the word *mnemonic*?

"*My* neighbor eats *mounds* of *neopolitan* ice cream."

How can you remember the colors of the rainbow?

Richard Of York Gave Battle In Vain
(ROYGBIV, i.e., red, orange, yellow, green, blue, indigo, violet)

The most often used mnemonics are made of expressions or words, such as the physical laws dealing with gases:

Boyle's law: At constant temperature, pressure is inversely proportional to volume.
Boyle's law is best of all because it presses gases awfully small.
The order of operations for math is Parentheses, Exponents, Multiply, Divide, Add, and Subtract = *Please Excuse My Dear Aunt Sally.*
The categories in the classification of life are Kingdom, Phylum, Class, Order, Family, Genus, Species = Kids Prefer Cheese Over Fried Green Spinach

Mnemonics do have some important cognitive characteristics: They are not simply techniques or tricks but rather imply the development of new structures. Remember that with cognitive strategies, our goal is to transform what we are learning so that we can facilitate other aspects of learning.

Mnemonics are strategies for encoding information with the purpose of making it more memorable. Thus, mnemonics create suggestion structures (like hints) made up of images or words in rhymes that will serve as mediators between a stimulus (word/image) to kick off another word, concept, or idea. The essence of the mnemonic is to link information we want to remember with one or more support mechanisms. Sometimes the more elaborate and even sillier are the mnemonics, the more effective they are.

While mnemonics are usually used for words, as all the examples above demonstrate, they also can be used for remembering small groups of numbers. For example, a number I often have to use is 11.434.217.0. The mnemonic is $1 + 1 = 2$, $434/2 = 217$, and 0 is left over. The license plate numbers on my car are 74209: $7 + 4 = 11$, and $2 + 0 + 9 = 11$ (so my license plate is 1111). There are two positive aspects of this kind of mnemonic. First, the amount of mental effort required is enough to create a lasting memory, and, second, the storage units are unique, belonging to the person who created them.

Visual Structures, Concept Maps, and Conceptual Networks

The extension of the idea of grouping by adding visual representation, highlighting relations, making links more evident, and improving structures leads to visual structures, concept maps, and conceptual networks, all of which help develop better mental structure and ensure stronger learning.

I spoke above of grouping ideas, concepts, and information by organizing and linking the information and ideas into units, such as "part/whole" or "higher/lower," or into a "chain of events." Extending the concept into maps and visual structures is an even more powerful strategy for learning.

The purpose of the map or graphic structure is to highlight relations between elements of what your child is learning. The conceptual or procedural map is a logical form for developing structure. It is the essence of a structure. The maps serve as visual stimuli that help your child create, store, and transfer simple and even complex organizations of information, increasing the probability of remembering, applying, and transferring the learned information in future learning events and in real-life applications.

To illustrate the idea of maps, let us start with a simple concept map about plants (see figure 3.8).

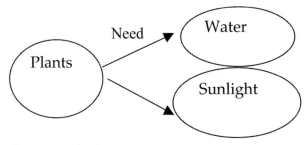

Figure 3.8. Simple Concept Map

Then we follow with a slightly more complex map, called a network tree map (see figure 3.9).

A concept map is more complex but is still understandable to a child of six to eight years of age. A general model of a concept map is presented in figure 3.10.

Learning concepts and their relations to other concepts and elements of a knowledge structure is a fundamental part of acquiring information. Concepts are often divided into two classes: concrete and abstract or defined. A concrete concept is one that can be defined entirely by the physical, perceptual features (appearance, sound, smell, and so on) of the object or event. It can be perceived by the five senses. An abstract or defined concept is one that is discriminated on the basis of its properties and is a generalized idea of a thing or class of things.

The basic components of the map are the following (see figure 3.11):

- The identifying elements or characteristics
- The context of the concept
- The concept
- Concrete examples of the concept (sometimes called substantiations)

Now let us apply this idea to a concrete example: a chair (see figure 3.12).

This is a clear example, but it is also useful because, as you will realize, the chair, while quite concrete, allows for many different interpretations, as furniture designers have developed thousands of variations on the concept of a chair, including even a big ball or a beanbag.

Now let us look at a defined or abstract concept. To get started, think about the concepts "aunt" and "uncle." These are great examples of a defined concept. If you point to a person and say, "That is my aunt," you will have labeled but not defined the concept. You must specify the correct characteristics; that is, a person who is either a sister or a brother of my father or my mother can be an aunt or an uncle.

A look at a more complex abstract concept will help us understand concepts and the idea of concept mapping. Remember that while concrete concepts have physical referents, abstract concepts have to be defined by characteristics that are not available to the senses. Examples of defined concepts include the following (see figure 3.13):

- Identifying all the lawyers described in a story using a definition
- Classifying governments as democracies using a definition

Think about love, for example. Other examples include freedom, crime, happiness, sadness, anger, work, hope, home, help, cowardice, confusion, friendship, greed, and innocence.

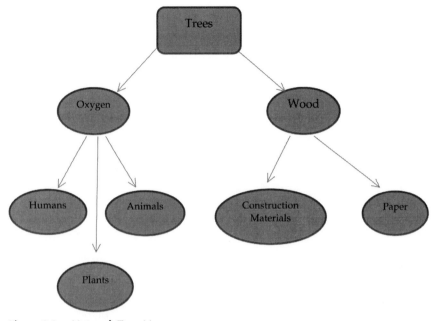

Figure 3.9. Network Tree Map

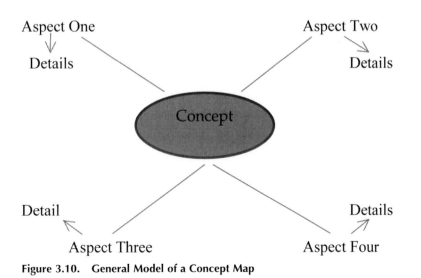

Figure 3.10. General Model of a Concept Map

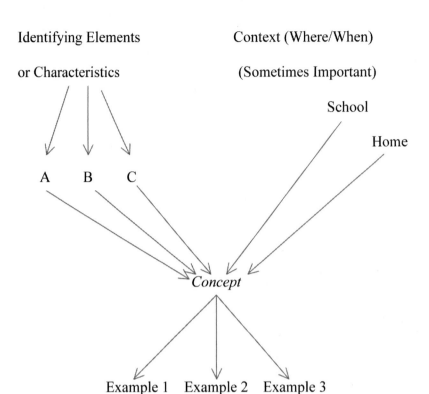

Figure 3.11.   **Components of a Concept Map**

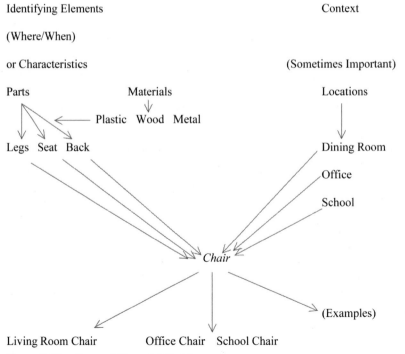

Figure 3.12.   **Concept Map of "Chair"**

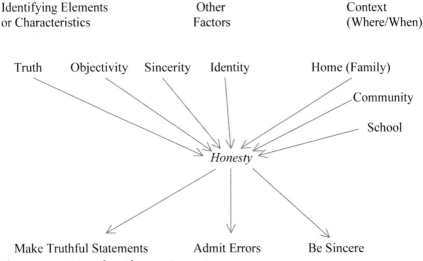

Identifying Elements or Characteristics   Other Factors   Context (Where/When)

Truth   Objectivity   Sincerity   Identity   Home (Family)

Community

School

Honesty

Make Truthful Statements   Admit Errors   Be Sincere

Figure 3.13.   Map of an Abstract Concept

Now, for a little fun, see how we can create a map to analyze the concept of Santa Claus (see figure 3.14). This is a descriptive map, and it is organized differently than the examples we have seen so far, but you should be able to identify all the parts.

It is easy to see how this map can help your child understand a little more and in a more organized manner the idea behind Santa Claus, his relation to good and bad, and the presents he will bring to children who are good. Learning to look at relations in this way is a major step toward developing a cognitive strategy for facilitating the learning of structure.

It will not surprise you that there are several types of maps, with differing organizations used for diverse purposes.

A circular map is very good for helping to define words, concepts, and things within a context.

A bubble map is useful to describe logical, emotional, or sensory qualities. A double bubble map helps facilitate comparison and contrast. Here is the graphic concept. This is a good map when you want your child to compare and contrast two ideas, concepts, or examples. Figure 3.15 shows the framework of a double bubble.

Figure 3.16 shows a simple example of the application of the double bubble map.

Figure 3.17 shows a more elaborate version of a concept map that links ideas to explain a relatively difficult concept: the length of days.[8]

Table 3.2 is tree map that shows relations between principle and subordinate ideas.

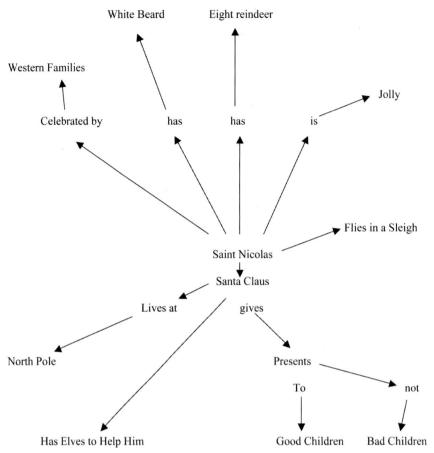

Figure 3.14. Concept Map of Santa Claus Story

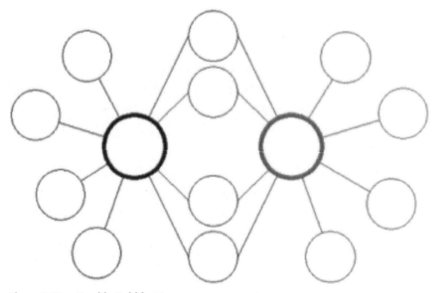

Figure 3.15. Double Bubble Map

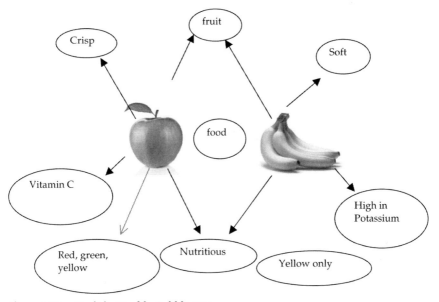

Figure 3.16. Fruit in Double Bubble Map

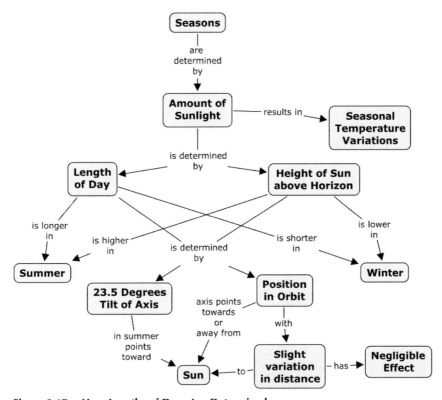

Figure 3.17. How Lengths of Days Are Determined

Table 3.2. Tree Map

Animals	
Wild	*Domesticated*
Monkeys	Cats
Baboons	Dogs
Lemurs	Horses
Apes	Hamsters
Gorillas	Cows
Orangutans	

This kind of map or chart is useful in biology, where much of the organization is hierarchical. Remember our mnemonic: Kids Prefer Cheese Over Fried Green Spinach.

A flow map is useful when you want to show how events occur in a sequence. Figure 3.18 shows a simple example of an everyday event: brushing one's teeth.

To an adult, this chart may seem obvious, but to a child, it can be a major step in beginning to form ideas about structure and sequence. The basic principle is that whatever schemes, visual structures, prompts, and supports you can give to your child will become important parts of ways to organize information.

Figure 3.19 shows a slightly different flowchart that simply adds the possibility of making a decision during the process of responding to the morning alarm clock.

Another example of a cause-and-effect chart is shown in figure 3.20. Both children want the toy, and this causes a dispute. A parent intervenes and negotiates some settlement (effect).

Another example is shown in figure 3.21, which is a hierarchical concept map explaining how beginning students may learn basic numerical concepts.

As a final example, look at this hierarchical flowchart in figure 3.22, which describes the steps a young child should

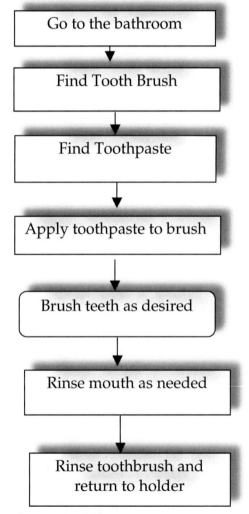

Figure 3.18. A Flow Map

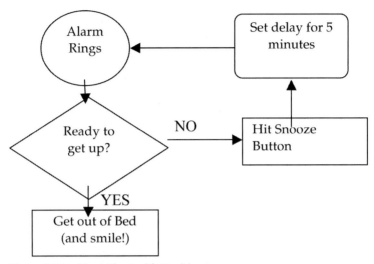

Figure 3.19.   Flow Chart with Decisions

follow to learn to read words. This chart is read "bottom up," which means that you start interpreting it at the bottom and move up through higher levels of learning to get to the final goal of reading words. The charts shown in figures 3.21 and 3.22 are good examples of truly sophisticated concept maps.

Most of the concepts maps are relatively simple to create and use for basic ideas. As a parent, you should learn a little about them (you probably have seen them often and in various settings) and then introduce your child to the maps when the appropriate occasion occurs. For example,

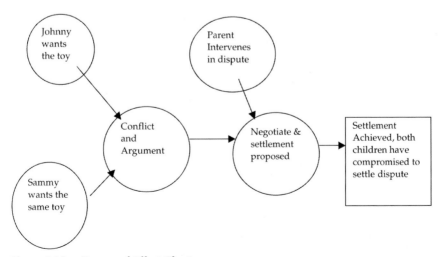

Figure 3.20.   Cause and Effect Chart

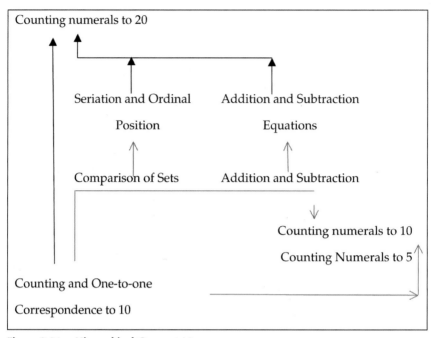

Figure 3.21. Hierarchical Concept Map

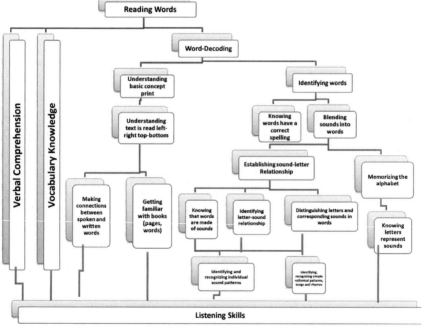

Figure 3.22. Hierarchical Map of Beginning Reading

if your child asks you to explain why something happens, you can and should map it. If your child asks you to elaborate an idea or concept, you can create a simple map to explain it. Also, if your child asks you for an explanation that is not immediately easy, you can Google the idea. The Internet is full of dozens of sources for information about mapping. Two places to begin could be http://www.inspiration.com and http://www.graphic.org/goindex.html.

In learning to comprehend what your child is reading, there are structures, sometimes called grammars, that provide influence in organizing and understanding written information.

Concept maps are useful in subjects that require learning many ideas and their relations. History, literature, language development, and beginning science are good subjects for applying concept maps. Initially, you may show existing maps from textbooks or other sources to your child so she may become familiar with the idea of mapping. Then you will want to show your child how to create concept maps and when to do so. As soon as possible, allow her to participate in mapping and try to increase her level of participation.

Research has shown that creating a map is almost twice as effective (in terms of learning) as simply reading an existing map. Creating a map with someone else (a classmate, sibling, parent, and so on) is even more effective.

There are three main reasons that concept maps are effective.

First, mapping shows the concepts and the relations between them, and this could help your child assimilate new information and hold it in a structured form. Remember that structured information is much easier to recover and use in problem solving.

Second, more mental effort is required to create the map than to simply read a passage or a list of concepts, meaning that there is better depth of processing the information, leading to better storage in long-term memory and a higher probability of recovering the information when needed.

Third, the map facilitates storage in two forms. The basic verbal information is stored in the semantic (words) memory, and the map as an image is stored in the eidetic or image memory. That means that your child has stored the information in two places, significantly increasing the possibility of recovering and using it when necessary as well as strengthening the underlying structure of the knowledge.

Learning from Narrative Stories. Networks can also be applied in learning information that we could call procedural, permitting the child to make things more concrete. When the child uses a network to record procedural information, the network normally includes indications of content, the required sequences, and the procedures. An example is shown in figure 3.23.

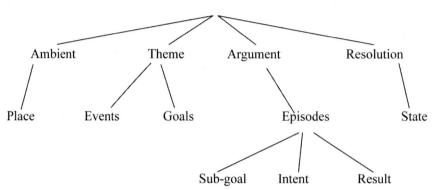

Figure 3.23.   Structural Network For a Story

Another schematic for stories that is quite similar is this one:

Story
Major Setting << Minor setting (context)
Initiating events >> Internal responses (goals, plans)
Action attempts >> Direct consequences >> Reactions

These two schemes are simple layouts of the elements involved in the typical story. In both schemes, there is an implied movement from left to right and top to bottom, that is, place, then theme, then argument, and finally resolution. When you read stories to your child, attempt to help him see these elements and how they flow in the story.

Table 3.3.

Story Element	Definition	Example
Setting	Introduction of main characters	Once upon a time there were three bears who lived in a house in the forest . . .
Initiating event	Action or dilemma or problem	One day a little girl named Goldilocks came by the house . . .
Response	Protagonist's reaction	She was surprised to see the house was empty . . .
Attempt	Action plan to address the problem	She ate baby bear's soup and broke his chair . . .
Consequence	Result of the action	Bears return to find damage and Goldilocks asleep.
Reaction	Response by protagonist	Bears wake her and she runs away.

In third and fourth grade, students are required to learn how to comprehend information presented to them in narrative and expository units (stories or explanations). Most students learn to understand information given in stories, primarily because they have been exposed to stories from early on. Mother read stories to them when they were babies. Even given that background, many children do need assistance in comprehending the more complex aspects of stories. The charts shown in figures 3.22 and 3.23 are examples of story "grammars," a term meant to convey and explain how stories are organized and what your child should be looking for when reading narrative texts (see table 3.3).

To help your child master the grammar of a story, you should move from simply reading stories with her to asking her to identify the key elements of the story. It is easy to start by asking about location and setting then identifying key persons. After a little practice, you may move on to the argument or problem: What is this story about? At this point, you will want to use several questions to help your child get a good grasp of what is going on.

Depending on the progress being made, you may want to start with relatively simple stories, probably ones that you have read to her before, and, as she begins to show understanding, move on to more complex stories. Go back to the list of questions on page 51. These can be your guide.

One good place to start to help your child understand narratives and extract meaning from them is with fables like those of Aesop. *The Boy Who Cried Wolf, The City Mouse and the Country Mouse, The Fox and the Grapes,* and *The Hare and the Tortoise* are all great stories from which your child can learn both the lesson of the story and the nature of narrative. Also, bookstores are full of stories written specifically for today's children.

Learning from Expository Texts. Learning to understand expository texts is somewhat similar but also more difficult. Again, the issue is to help your child learn to identify the structure, the "grammar," of the expository text. There is considerable research showing that understanding structure significantly improves a child's ability to comprehend the exposition.

Passages are easier to remember when they have a clear organizational structure. Initially, most students are unaware of text structure. That is to be expected since most of them will not have had the concept presented to them, nor will they have discovered it through their reading. They may not have learned it in school.

In this area of learning strategies, there are two main structural forms to be mastered: description and collection. A descriptive text, as you can imagine, presents information about a topic, such as the following:

The Olympic Games are the leading international sporting event featuring summer and winter competitions in which thousands of athletes from more than 200 nations compete.[9]

A collective exposition gives a number of descriptions, attributes, or settings joined together:

> There are many different events that occur in the Olympics. There are the major ceremonies like the opening event and the closing ceremonies. Then there are pure competitions like races, games, jumping competitions. There are team competitions like gymnastics, archery, fencing and others. There is even synchronized swimming.[10]

Both descriptive and collective grammars present information primarily without asking the reader to perform analytic actions.

When attempting to derive meaning from expository texts, your child can use a few simple steps:

- Identify the author's purpose and conclusions:
  - What is he trying to say?
  - What is he trying to convince you?
- Identify the author's premises; on what did he base his exposition?
  - Are the premises believable?
- Did the author use inductive or deductive reasoning?
- Does the conclusion reached by the author logically follow from the premises?

Following these steps should help your child significantly. It is probable that you will have to help and to model the use of these steps so that your child can learn and appreciate them.

ADVANCED LEARNING STRATEGIES

Comparison and Contrast

When a child (or any person) looks for relations between events, facts, ideas, or concepts through a parallel examination of two or more of these, she is using a form of processing (and a cognitive strategy) called comparison. What this means is to highlight aspects in such a form as to facilitate discovery of similarities and differences between the things being observed. Compare and contrast is the process of identifying how things are alike and different. Comparison refers to how two or more things are alike; contrast refers to how they are different.

Comparison and contrast help build stronger mental structures because they lead your child to examine more closely the events or concepts and to identify those aspects that differentiate one from another. This effort increases the amount of logical connections with the structure of the idea or concept that your child is learning. The amount of mental effort invested helps solidify the structures the child is developing and also prepares conditions for subsequent transfer of what has been learned to new situations, such as problem solving.

Human nature leads us to use comparison and contrast. From a very young age, we compare things and evaluate them along different criteria. Children compare foods and drinks from a very early age, deciding which they like and which they do not like. They compare toys, clothes, friends, and other people and decide which or whom they prefer. Comparing is natural, and when we develop it as a cognitive strategy, it can be effective in facilitating new learning.

One way to get started is by looking at synonyms and antonyms. The process requires comparing and contrasting. Children from eight or nine years of age can learn this quickly, and it prepares them to do more extensive comparison-and-contrast work. Ask your child to generate synonyms for simple words, such as *talk, allow, correct, tall, task, gentle,* and *awful,* several times on several different days. When you are talking and an opportunity arises, ask for a synonym. Then do the same with antonyms, such as *narrow, quiet, big, many,* and *plain.* Make a game of it:

"Oh, what was that word? Can you think of a similar word?"

The first step is to recognize two or more concepts or objects and identify what characteristics they have in common, listing them, for example, in a column. The second step is to identify the major differences between them, again listing them in a column. The result could be shown in two columns, one for similarities and another for differences between the objects.

For example, look back at the double bubble chart shown in figure 3.16:

- Both apples and bananas are fruit.
- Both are foods.
- Both can be made into juice or cakes.
- Both grow on trees.

Comparison is the process of identifying how things are alike and different. Comparing requires children to think about the specific attributes or characteristics of the thing that they're observing and studying. Comparing promotes vocabulary development, concept development, and higher-level thinking.

Think of a simple comparison appropriate for a child of five to seven years of age, such as a baby duck and a baby chicken. What do both have in common? Lead your child to recognize things, such as that both are birds, both are small, both have feet and wings, and both have a very similar shape, feathers, tails, and so on.

Then ask your child to identify what is different about them. The duck's feet are different. The duck's bill is different. The duck can swim, and the chicken cannot. The chicken can walk fast, while the duck waddles. The duck is more comfortable in the water. Don't tell these things to your child. Tease them out and make him discover the differences. Guide with questions. Are the duck's feet different than those of the chicken? What sounds do the two birds make?

Comparing and contrasting help your child develop a cognitive strategy that will assist her to mentally organize the information she is learning.

Teaching strategies that have been found effective in coaching the compare-and-contrast text structure include the following:

- Teaching the vocabulary that signals the compare-and-contrast structures. Some compare signal words are *similar, like, still, likewise, in the same ways, in comparison, at the same time,* and *in the same manner.*
- Some contrast signal words are *however, on the other hand, but, yet, nevertheless, conversely, rather, on the contrary, nonetheless, in contrast.*
- Teaching the two general kinds of compare-and-contrast structures:
  1. The whole-to-whole (divided) pattern of comparison (A + B); that is, the first thing is discussed in entirety, and then the second thing is discussed.
  2. The part-to-part (alternating) pattern of comparison (A/B + A/B); that is, elements of the first thing are discussed, then similar elements of the second are discussed. This process is then repeated.

When you compare items, you look for their similarities—the things that make them the same—and their differences, the things that discriminate them.

Finally, comparing is a strategy that supports learning in all subjects when two or more similar items in a category can be compared. Categories might include places, historical events, animal groups, planets, famous people, modes of transportation, systems of the body, diseases, types of clouds, and so on. The categories become part of the child's mental structure, and the comparisons strengthen and amplify the structures.

Sometimes it is useful to create a comparison chart that will facilitate the identification of similarities and differences. Table 3.4 gives a simple example.

A number of instructional strategies help children develop an understanding of what comparison is and use that concept of comparison to support learning, reading, and writing. These strategies can be used by parents in real-world situations or by teachers in instructional situations.

Table 3.4. Units to Be Compared

Aspects	Pine Tree	Rose	Elephant	Lion	Shark
Body features	Tall, many branches		Large, thick skin, trunk		Medium to large, thick skin, fin
Habitat		Garden		Savannah	Ocean
Energy sources			Grass		Fish

Further, some of the strategies can help children write reports, comprehend while they're reading, or study for tests.

Table 3.5 gives examples of comparisons you can teach your child at different age levels.

In relation to reading comprehension, as we mentioned above, there are grammars for narrative and expository texts. One of the expository grammars is comparison, where the reader is required to organize information and concepts on the basis of similarities and differences.

ANALOGIES, SIMILES, AND METAPHORS

Analogy, simile, and metaphor agree in designating a comparison between things essentially or generically different but strikingly alike in one or more pertinent aspects. Analogy is the general term given that similes and metaphors are kinds of analogies. Analogy is usually limited in its use to a comparison that brings out the likeness between two things for the sake of elucidating something hard to understand. For example, God cannot be described except by analogy.

A simile is an imaginative analogy generally used for literary effects by carrying over the emotion aroused by one image or idea to the other with which it is being compared. "She's as fierce as a tiger."

Similes and metaphors are ways to compare and contrast. To differentiate between the two, here's a quick, hard-to-forget way to tell them apart: Similes use comparison words (e.g., *like* or *as*), and metaphors don't:

The sun is like a big orange in the sky. (simile)
The sun is a big orange in the sky. (metaphor)

Similes and metaphors are used to compare two nouns and also make some contrasting statements between the two words. To clarify, simile and metaphor are used to show comparison between two nouns in either a positive or a negative way. However, metaphor never uses *like* or *as* when comparing two words.

A metaphor differs from a simile because it does not explicitly state the analogy but imaginatively identifies one object with another and ascribes

Table 3.5. Examples of Comparisons at Different Ages

3 to 5 years	6 to 8 years	9 to 11 years	12+ years
Shoes to sandals	Weeds to flowers	Christopher Columbus to early astronauts	Halloween night to prom night
Cheerios to Corn Flakes	The decisions of Red Riding Hood to the decisions of Goldilocks	School bullies to dictators	Your best friend to your archenemy
Apple juice to orange juice	Making an apple pie to making a mud pie	Hurricanes to blizzards	Being the president to being a homeless person
Toy cars to dolls	Spending time with your friend to spending time with your dog	Acting to lying	Being a snob to being a nerd
	Snowfall to rainfall	Being afraid to being bored	Writing essays to going to the dentist
	Living on a farm to living in the city	Going to a movie to watching a movie at home	The influence of music to the influence of books
	Washing dishes to washing laundry		Physical beauty to inner beauty
	The life of a dog to the life of a cat	A female friend and a male friend	Working as a waitress to working as a flight attendant
	The Three Bears to The Three Little Pigs	Your happiest day to your saddest day	Talking to your mom and talking to your friends

to the first one more of the qualities of the second one. For example, "Those who don't study are cattle dressed in men's clothing" does not say that they are *like* cows; it says that they *are* cattle.

"He was drowning in paperwork" is a metaphor in which having to deal with a lot of paperwork is being compared to drowning in an ocean of water. Note it says "he was," not "as if he was."

Here are some examples of similes:

- "He was *like* a cock who thought the sun had risen to hear him crow." (George Eliot, *Adam Bede*)
- "Human speech is *like* a cracked cauldron on which we bang out tunes that make bears dance, when we want to move the stars to pity." (Gustave Flaubert, *Madame Bovary*)
- "Humanity, let us say, is *like* people packed in an automobile which is traveling downhill without lights at terrific speed and driven by a four-year-old child. The signposts along the way are all marked 'Progress.'"
(Lord Dunsany)
- "Life is *like* an onion: You peel it off one layer at a time, and sometimes you weep."
(Carl Sandburg)
Shrek: Ogres are *like* onions.
Donkey: They stink?
Shrek: Yes. No!
Donkey: They make you cry?
Shrek: No!
Donkey: You leave them out in the sun, they get all brown, start sprouting little white hairs.
Shrek: No! Layers! Onions have layers!
(*Shrek*, 2001)

Here is an example that can help you visualize what figures of speech can do. Common expressions such as "falling in love," "wracking our brains," "hitting a sales target," and "climbing the ladder of success" are all metaphors, the most pervasive figure of all. Similes are imaginative analogies used for literary effect when making explicit comparisons ("light as a feather") or impact ("the news hit her like a bucket of cold water") and hyperbole to emphasize a point ("I'm starving!," "It's raining cats and dogs!," "I've told you a million times not to exaggerate!"). Other examples are the following:

"Love is an ideal thing, marriage a real thing." (Goethe)

"It was the best of times, it was the worst of times, it was the age of wisdom, it was the age of foolishness, it was the epoch of belief, it was the epoch of incredulity, it was the season of Light, it was the season of Darkness, it was the spring of hope, it was the winter of despair, we had everything before us, we had nothing before us, we were all going direct to Heaven, we were all going direct the other way." (Charles Dickens, *A Tale of Two Cities*)

"You're easy on the eyes, Hard on the heart." (Terri Clark)

More examples of metaphors are the following:

- The mind is barren soil, and will produce no crop, unless it is continuously fertilized with foreign matter.
- These tuition fees are hardly as expensive as the teacher called Experience.
- The richest genius, like the most fertile soil, when uncultivated shoots up the rankest weeds.
- Knowledge doesn't keep any better than fish.
- There comes a leap in consciousness, call it insight, and the solution comes to you, and you don't know how or why.
- Natural abilities are like natural plants that need pruning by study.
- Minds are like parachutes; they only function when they are open.
- Conversation enriches the understanding but solitude is the school of genius.

(The last statement has research support. One famous psychologist studied the lives of several geniuses. The only thing he found that they had in common was that all of them had spent some significant amount of time in their youth in relative solitude.)

To teach your child to recognize and subsequently develop metaphors, you should do the following:

- Show her a model of the process (with lots of examples):
  - The Internet is an information superhighway.
  - The Internet is a giant flea market.
  - The Internet is a coffee shop.
  - The Internet is a huge newspaper.
- Use familiar content when starting to learn.
- Use graphic organizers (e.g., charts) to demonstrate aspects of metaphors.
- Help your child to identify what is most important in the component from which the metaphor is to be developed.
- Prompt your child to look for patterns in the components.

Then present simple examples drawn from your own context and ask your child to complete them:

- Sickness is _____.
- The brain is _____.
- The Great Wall of China is_____.
- The Sahara Desert is_____.

The analogy strategy uses comparison to help children learn new information. The purpose is to highlight comparisons in order to clarify aspects that are not always easy to understand. This strategy relates the new information to something that the child already understands. Typically, analogies look for relations between pairs of concepts, such as *happy* is to *sad* as *big* is to *small* (*happy* and *big* are the opposites of *sad* and *small*). The features of a good analogy are following:

- Based on an exact or similar idea
- Simplicity
- Embodies the concept or relationship between things clearly

The process for teaching how to understand and even create analogies is just like the process for learning metaphors:

- Show him a model of the process (with lots of examples):
  - *Caterpillar* is to *butterfly* as *tadpole* is to *frog*.
  - *Whale* is to *mammal* as *snake* is to *reptile*.
  - *Brain* is to *human* as *central processor* is to *computer*.
  - *Gasoline* is to the *automobile* as *electricity* is to the *television*.
- Use familiar content when starting to learn.
- Use graphic organizers (e.g., charts) to demonstrate aspects of metaphors.

- Help your child to identify what is most important in the component from which the metaphor is to be developed.
- Prompt your child to look for patterns in the components.

Give your child examples of cases in which one of the four components is missing and ask her to deduce the missing component:

Evaporation is to *steam* as _____ is to *liquid*.
Trees are to *forest* as *grass* is to _____.
Office is to *working* as _____ is to *cooking*.
Fish is to _____ as *bird* is to *air*.
A gang of boys is like a pack of _____.
The sword is the weapon of a warrior, while the _____ is the weapon
of a writer.

The following example shows how a child's experiences with an orange can help him learn about the layers of the earth. You could even peel an orange while sharing this analogy to help your child conceptualize the information:

The earth is a lot like an orange. The earth's crust is like the peel of an orange. The soil and rocks that make up the earth's crust cover the earth just like the peel covers the orange. The peel of an orange is quite thin. The crust of the earth, however, ranges from three miles thick under the deepest parts of the ocean to twenty-two miles thick under mountain peaks. Underneath the orange peel is the sweet juicy fruit that we like to eat. The earth's mantle is under the earth's crust.

While the juicy sections of the orange are cool, the earth's mantle is a layer of very hot, sometimes molten rock. The juicy part of the orange is thick; the mantle is also a very thick part of the earth—about 1,800 miles thick. Finally, the orange usually has seeds in the middle of it. The middle of the orange is like the earth's core. The earth's core has two parts: an outer core made up of molten rock and a solid inner core. The core has a radius of 2,100 miles.[11]

Use of Inferences

To infer means to draw conclusions not explicitly stated based on evidence and reasoning. A group of closely related concepts are inference, deduction, conclusion, and judgment. They are applied to propositions and mental formulations derived by reasoning.

Infer means to draw an opinion, a principle, a fact, a probability, or something similar from the evidence presented or the assumption accepted. In simple terms, inference is the ability to use two or more pieces of information to arrive at a third piece of information that is implicit.

Deduce means to infer with an implication of very definite grounds for the inference. Sometimes the deduction is from specific facts to general concepts and sometimes vice versa:

All animals have RNA.
A rat is an animal.
Therefore, a rat has DNA.

Conclude is roughly equivalent to *deduce*, and it means to draw the inference that the conclusion is the necessary consequence of preceding propositions.

Judgment generally connotes careful examination of evidence and critical testing of premises and the fitness of the conclusion for affirmation.

All these words form a constellation of processes and results related to the attempt to establish veracity, certainty, and truth. As a cognitive learning strategy, they form the highest level of learning, which is crucial for your child to achieve if you want her to be a truly good thinker.

Try this story out on your seven-, eight-, or nine-year-old:

A rooster is on the side of a road, scratching and searching for seeds or little bugs to eat. He does not find any, so he decides to cross to the other side of the road. As he is crossing, he hears a very loud sound and feels the road shake under his feet. He does not make it to the other side. What happened?

Most children can deduce what happened. If they cannot immediately, a hint (e.g., what was the sound?) will usually lead them to the answer.

Learning inferences can begin as early as seven or eight years of age. For example, language implies results. Look at these questions:

"He rode his bike." Was it a boy or a girl?
"Please bait my hook." Am I playing basketball?
"Sorry! I broke it." Could that be a stuffed toy?
"The little lamb lost its mother." Who is its mother?
"I see a thousand stars." What time of the day is it?
"He threw a snowball at me!" What time of the year is it?
"Breakfast is ready." What time of the day is it?

The idea is to realize that inference can be developed from rather early if it is done correctly. Always look for simple situations where an inference is possible and ask your child to resolve it. Do it often.

You can cue your child to infer by asking simple questions:

What is your guess about this?
Could it be that . . .

What could this mean?
Perhaps this is the right way . . .

Inference and deduction help build stronger mental structures because they lead your child to examine more closely the propositions and evidence to support or deny them. The amount of mental effort invested helps to solidify the structures your child is developing and also prepares conditions for subsequent transfer of what has been learned to new situations.

Nature is deterministic and certain, but for humans it is often uncertain. Our primary way to understand the world is through inferences, which have to do more with predicting probabilities than with demonstrative proofs. Our ability to make inferences depends mainly on two components. These are the nature and limitations of the human mind and the structure of the environments in which the mind operates. Because of the mind's limitations (particularly the fragility of working memory), we often use approximate methods to handle tasks.

Our minds have many specific learning tracks that prepare us to expect and anticipate certain kinds of situations and to understand them by making rich inferences drawn from particular information patterns. Our minds are bundles of expectations, preferences, and habits of inference organized to obtain the largest amount of results with the smallest amount of processing (remember that working memory is small). Our minds exist to predict what will happen in the future.

Our abilities to make inferences are impressive. Most often, we make unconscious inferences about what is going on and what will happen. But in the case of academic study and the development of critical thinking, we can teach our children to improve their ability to infer, to deduce, to judge, and to evaluate.

If the family is sitting down at the dining room table, waiting for dinner, and they hear a crash and the sound of broken glass in the kitchen, all of them can infer what has happened. That kind of inference may be thought of as "gap filling." We get partial knowledge, but it is enough for us to fill in the gap.

Inference comes naturally to us: It is part of our genetic inheritance. Without the capability to infer, to deduce, and to make judgments, we would not have survived as a species. Inference is like comparing and contrasting, like memorizing, and like asking questions, all of which are natural. In an effort to help your child become a good thinker, you want to take the natural responses and improve them as much as possible.

Parents should model inference. This is done through "thinking aloud" practices, talking about what one is observing or reading so your child can experience what you are elaborating:

"Let's see, this sentence says that the bear was very hungry. What will he likely do?"

"Oh, the car is going very fast and the brakes are not good. What might happen?"

"It is very cloudy and windy. What should we expect?"

Background factors, as always, are very important. The more background information your child has, the easier it is to make inferences. The better your child can read, the easier it is to make inferences. The more you talk to your child, the more you make observations and ask questions, the better your child will be able to make inferences.

In the course of discussion about inference events, the main question you want to ask is "How do you know?" You ask questions about relationships between characters, goals, and motivations, questions such as "Why did the chicken cross the road?"

You want to ask questions about comprehension, such as "Is there information that does not agree with what we already know?" That is a very important question because it requires that your child confront what he knows with what new information is being presented.

As a general idea, when talking about the world around them and when reading new information, you want to ensure that your child is always asking "why" questions. How? You ask them so that your child learns to ask them.

Some more typical questions that require your child to draw inferences include "What action does this thing or person usually perform?"

- How is this thing usually used? (a tennis racquet, a piano, a car)
- What is the process for making this thing? (a tennis racquet, a piano, a car)
- What particular taste, feel, or smell does this thing have? (a boiled egg, a mango, sulfuric acid)
- What particular emotional state does the person feel? (a sports person after winning or losing a race)
- How does this action change the size or shape of the thing? (a flood, an earthquake)

In reading comprehension, inference is a major part of problem solving, which we will see in more detail in chapter 7.

A WORD ABOUT PRACTICE

Practice is important for teaching and learning.

Practice greatly increases the likelihood that your child will permanently remember new information encountered by moving it into long-term memory. Practice increases automaticity, which means learning to apply elements of knowledge automatically without thinking about them. Automaticity is achieved only through extensive rehearsal and repetition, and it frees up cognitive resources to handle more challenging tasks. Skills and knowledge that have been learned to the automatic level do not use space in working memory, leaving room for other thinking elements.

When students practice solving problems, it appears that they increase their ability to transfer practiced skills to new and more complex problems.[12] Sufficient practice helps students acquire expertise in a subject matter or skill area. Equally important, cognitive gains from practice often bring about motivation for more learning.[13]

As a parent, you should think of practice not as rote repetition but as deliberate, goal-directed rehearsal paired with reflection on problem-solving processes. When your child is practicing identifying phonemes, the ultimate goal is for her to read with fluency and comprehension. Although fluent reading may be too complex a task for beginning readers to tackle, the more manageable task of identifying phonemes may "frame" a child's learning to achieve the ultimate goal of reading. You should design practice activities with the goal of transferring knowledge to new and more complex problems in mind.

Feedback is most effective when it contains descriptions of how the child's work meets performance criteria and what she can do to improve. This kind of descriptive feedback is more effective than feedback consisting of vague, general comments (e.g., "nice work" or "needs improvement"). Feedback should also be focused on the learning process. That is, parents should focus their feedback on helping their children reflect on their problem-solving skills as well as on progress they have made.

To summarize and facilitate the use of the cognitive strategies, table 3.6 lists the strategies and explains what can be expected or what can be most logically developed at different age levels.

Table 3.6. Progression of Learning Cognitive Strategies

Strategy	3 to 5 years	6 to 8 years	9 to 11 years	12+ years
Memorization	Basic and important as child begins to construct schemes.	Important as child continues to construct schemes while beginning to use strategies.	Less important as child should be using strategies to facilitate learning.	Less important as teen should be relying primarily on strategies for learning.
Paraphrasing	Initially good, but child must learn what is correct and what is not.	Child is getting better and knows when to use strategy.	Much better but also opportunities to paraphrase may be dropping.	Usually has adopted the strategy and knows when to use it.
Questions	Use lots of basic questions.	Make questions more inferential.	Much more inferential; comparison and contrast.	Much more inferential, evaluative, analytic.
Verbal chains	Child develops simple chains.	Chains increase in complexity.	Further increase in complexity.	Teen should be building strong sense of logic.
Images	Child can use many images to help form schemes.	Child can use many images to help form schemes and structures.	Images become less important.	Images are less important.
Concept maps, charts, layouts	Child is beginning to develop concepts.	Increase use of concepts and the identification of relations (structure) and show maps.	Increase considerably. Should be able to make conceptual maps of most subjects being studied.	Should be a major strategy. Should be able to make conceptual maps of almost all subjects being studied.
Compare and contrast	Simple but often	More complex and more often	Even more complex and often	Should be a major strategy.
Inference	Just beginning, the mental structure is growing.	Your child can begin to infer and should be encouraged.	Inference should be a strong skill.	Inference should be a strong skill and major strategy.

FOUR

Metacognition: Awareness for Thinking

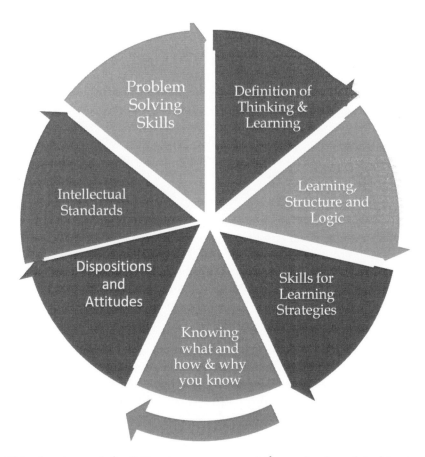

This chapter and the following one present three closely related topics: metacognition (also known as cognitive awareness), affective variables that influence human learning, and general dispositions, which are the affective issues taken to the point of action. These three topics form the basis for the propensity to act positively in learning and in subsequent performance. In this chapter, we focus on awareness as it relates specifically to learning new information.

KNOWING WHAT YOU KNOW: METACOGNITION

The Master said, shall I teach thee what is wisdom? To know what we know, and know what we do not know, is wisdom.

—Confucius

A key aspect of thinking is awareness: of what you are thinking, of why you are thinking, of how you are thinking, what you know and what you do not know, and where your thinking is or should be going. This awareness has been given a special name by psychologists. It is called metacognition, which means "cognition about cognition," or what you think about what you think. Metacognition is the ability to reflect on, understand, evaluate, and guide one's learning.

Research has established that the higher the levels of awareness a child has in early learning stages, the more effective and long lasting is the learning. This is important. The awareness allows and facilitates that the learner, your child, has more control over the process, has more knowledge of what she is learning, can more easily identify mistakes and correct them, and is aware of her rate of progress and other elements that clearly improve learning and achievement.

Accompanying what you know about what you know is the critical issue of what you want to do, what your child's motivation is, what his or her dispositions are, and how can you stimulate them. Knowing is important, but wanting to know, to do, and to achieve are even more important. Good thinking is not only a skill but also a set of attitudes (more on this in chapter 5).

Your child may learn quite well all the cognitive strategies presented in chapter 3. But knowing the strategies does not necessarily mean that she will use them. The key to selecting and using them is awareness of her knowledge and of her process of learning. If she is aware that she does not know something or that she does not know it well enough, she may search for a strategy to help her improve learning.

Metacognition includes a person's knowledge about the nature of people as thinkers, about the nature of different mental tasks, and about possible strategies that can be used to solve various mental tasks. Major emphasis has been on what is called metamemory, or what you know about what you know. This is knowledge about self and about knowledge and about available learning strategies. Also important is your child's knowledge about when, why, and how to use strategies to facilitate communication, perception and attention, general understanding, and problem solving.

This involves planning to learn, monitoring comprehension, and evaluating progress. Your child also needs to know how to use language and communication, perception, and attention in facilitating learning and have a general understanding of problem solving. Another word for metacognition is *mindfulness,* as when you say that your child is mindful of what she is doing, of what her duties and attitudes are, and so on. It is part of what Socrates was talking about when he said, "Know thyself."

Metacognition is the most powerful of the various cognitive and affective learning strategies you can teach your child. One researcher[1] has established that metacognition, awareness of what is known and how, can raise your child's achievement by as much as 20 percent. That is important. It also interacts closely with other aspects of thinking, and it is powerful.

WHAT YOU KNOW

It is important to be aware of what you know and do not know. Your child should be able to discriminate whether he knows some specific item of information from as early as three or four years of age, at least for basic information. From about age four, your child will begin to understand that what people think and believe as well as what they desire will affect how they act. Her ability to develop further awareness can easily be stimulated by good questioning:

- Did you know that . . . ?
- Can you see an image of . . . ?
- Do you remember . . . ?
- What do you know about . . . ?

Early in life, the child will often presume to know something she does not really know. Teachers see this frequently in the classroom when they ask who knows the answer to a question or who can define a concept or rule. Many children say they can: They may think they can, or they may be trying to respond to what they perceive as the teacher's expectations.

But then, when asked to fulfill the task, they often can do so only partially or not at all. They did not accurately evaluate and state their memory contents. But they can easily learn to measure their minds if they are encouraged by their parents using the right kinds of questions to stimulate them to think.

HOW YOU KNOW, HOW DO YOU LEARN, AND HOW DO YOU LIKE TO LEARN?

Do you prefer to learn new information by reading or by listening? When you read, do you underline or highlight important phrases or words? Do you draw little charts or graphs? Do you try to identify the key concepts? Do you write in the margins?

Children develop preferences for ways of learning, and these preferences influence how they desire to learn. The development of these preferences is important. For example, if you read books to your child from rather early in her life, she likely will develop a preference for learning through reading. If you allow her to watch a lot of television, she may develop a preference for learning through listening. If you combine a bit of both—reading and watching—she may develop a good attitude toward both reading and listening.

Think about your own case in terms of the question above. Do you prefer to read or to listen? Look around you. How many people you know are ones who prefer to listen rather than read? How many are ones who are constantly reading newspapers, magazines, and books and on the Internet? How many are listening to television or music or talking to other people a lot? Those are styles of learning that the people have adopted over time, mostly by accident, from family and environmental influences. What you do with your child can influence directly the style that your child learns and adopts.

In the initial stages of learning something new, your child will make better progress by establishing small goals:

- What is the topic, subject, or exercise to be learned?
- What do I know about this topic (from things I have learned before)?
- What do I expect to find out about the topic?
- What do I want to remember so that I can talk about it later?

Also, in the initial stages of learning, your child may feel insecure about what she is learning and may ask metacognitive questions, such as the following:

- Am I confused by this subject?
- Maybe I don't have enough information?

- Is there a word or words that I don't understand?
- Do I lack background in this subject?
- Do I understand the author's purpose?
- Am I focusing on the important information and organizing it?

Your child's attention can be drawn to various aspects of the learning process. The first could be how your child pays attention to what he is learning or simply to the world around him. The first step in learning is to pay attention to, attend to, and focus on the relevant stimuli in some form. This can be influenced by directing his attention toward things:

- Did you see that?
- Do you know where to look to find that?
- Are you listening closely?
- Can you hear that specific sound?
- What did it sound like?
- Where on the page is the word "X"?
- Can you find the best idea?
- Does the picture on the page help you to understand the story?
- Did you notice the sequences of those events?
- Did you slow down when you encountered new information?

From paying attention, your child should proceed to processing the new information in the fashion described in chapters 2 and 3. You can lead and prompt her with more questions, indications, guidance, modeling, and rewarding.

In the case of learning physical motor skills, the child's attention should be focused on the sequence of events and the shape of the responses. When learning to draw or write, for example, the parent wants to prompt with comments such as the following:

- Do you have a mental model of what you want to draw?
- Can you imagine what you want to draw?
- Do you have a picture that you are trying to copy?
- Have you examined the shape of the letters or forms you are trying to learn?

Then stimulate the child to practice, practice, practice because motor skills, by their nature, require lots of repetition.

The verbal elaboration category is very large, as you saw in chapter 3. To develop your child's awareness of the processes he is using when learning the major questions, some hints, guides, or reminders of how to do learning events can be used. The following are some examples.

In the case of verbal repetition, you may ask things like the following:

- Did you repeat that number, spelling, or series enough times?
- Can you remember the process or the rule well enough to repeat it?
- Are you pacing yourself while learning in order to have enough time?
- Are you good at organizing the information?

In learning through paraphrasing, the first question is whether what is being learned can be paraphrased. Then ask, How can you express that idea in your own words? Are you sure that way of saying the idea retains the original meaning? Can you give examples of other ways of stating the idea? Also, as in all the metacognitive encouragements, you will want to encourage your child to try harder, leading to more mental effort being placed into the learning event.

Look at a simple example of how metacognition works. I speak three languages: two of them well and one not so well. When I am speaking, reading, or writing in English, I do so automatically, without thinking about the process of speaking (I do think about the content). I do not use metacognition until I come to a problem, usually a failure to find the exact word I am looking for.

Then I become aware of the issue, and my mind moves away from automatic production and goes into a search mode until I find the word. Sometimes that requires looking at the dictionary or asking a friend or colleague for suggestions. Once the answer is found, I return to a normal pace of speaking, reading, or writing.

The same thing happens when I am speaking, writing, or reading Spanish, except that I probably have a few more problems occurring, more vocabulary issues, and maybe some minor grammar problems (like the past perfect subjunctive mood). I still speak in an automatic mode.

When I speak Portuguese, which I do not speak as well as Spanish, my cognitive self-awareness, my metacognition, is almost constantly turned on as I look for the correct words, attempt to choose the correct syntax and grammar, and review the pronunciation. So metacognition, once something is learned, functions like a backup system to help when problems arise.

A similar situation exists when a child is reading. As she moves through paragraphs, she will continue to read until she finds a word or concept that she does not understand. Then she should turn on her metacognition, stop, go back, and reread to make sure that she has grasped what has caused problems. Once the problem has been clarified, she may continue to read at a normal pace.

In the case of using questions in the learning process, you will want to stimulate awareness of how and what was asked through the main metacognitive questions:

- Did you ask yourself about this concept, problem, rule, or whatever?
- Did you ask yourself the right questions?
- How many questions did you ask?
- Were you able to answer the questions?

When your child is using grouping, chunking, and selective combination to learn the idea, you will want to remind him to pay attention to the techniques he is using to learn. Metacognitive questions should include things like the following:

- On what basis are you organizing the concepts? Part, whole, class, chain?
- Do you have enough information to organize the ideas in the way you are trying to do so?
- Are you using previous learning to help organize what is new?
- Is the organization helping you understand and remember the relations between the elements?

When your child is using images, episodes, or mnemonics in learning, you can imagine many questions to help increase her awareness of how she is using the images and what she is learning:

- What is in this image? What does it say to you?
- How does it relate to the concept, idea, or rule you are learning?
- How does the image remind you of the concept?
- How does the image relate to the schema or structure you are developing?
- When you have to memorize something new, do you construct mental images to help you remember?

When your child is using comparison and contrast, metaphors, and analogies in learning, you can imagine many questions to help increase his awareness of how he is using the images and what he is learning:

- How well did I do in making up comprehension questions?
- How well did I do in making up connection questions?
- Did you focus on the meaning and significance of new information?
- How well did I explain to others?
- How well did I discuss today's lesson?
- How well do I think I understand today's lesson?
- Did I summarize what I learned after I finished?

The well-developed awareness and metacognition of your child allows her to be "on track" with what she is learning, to be conscious of learning when it is necessary to be conscious, and to make comments like the following:

Table 4.1. Summary of Learning Strategies

Initial Learning Strategies	Major Metacognitive Questions
Attention strategies	Am I paying attention to the right thing?
Physical strategies	Do I know the correct sequence of movements?
	Am I repeating the sequence correctly?
Verbal elaboration strategies	
Repetition	Am I looking at the right information?
	Am I repeating it correctly?
	How many times do I need to repeat it?
	To what am I relating it?
Paraphrasing	Is this information appropriate for paraphrasing?
	How can I best paraphrase?
	Am I faithful to the meaning of the original statement?
Use of questions	What question should I ask?
	Do I know what, who, when, where, and why?
Grouping and selective combinations	What are the logical ways I can subdivide this information?
	How can this information be organized to make it easier to understand, grasp, and remember?
	Is the relation cause and effect?
Elaboration through images	
Images	Do I have an image of this idea or concept?
	What kind of image will help me remember and relate?
Structures and maps	Do I understand the structure and organization of this information?
	Can I make a concept or relational map of this information?
Mnemonics	Is a mnemonic available? How many times to repeat to memorize it?
	Can I make my own mnemonic?
Episodes	What is the sequence of the episodes? What are the main events?
	Can I visualize the events (images)?
Advanced learning strategies	
Comparison and contrast	How do I compare?
	What are the principal elements or features of each concept?
Use of inference	What information leads me to suspect a relation?
	What signals relations?
Application or future test	How and when can I use this in the future?
	Can I imagine future events where this knowledge will be useful?

- So far I've learned . . . (very important knowledge of progress)
- This made me think of . . .
- That didn't make sense (important awareness event)
- I think _____ will happen next.
- I reread that part because it was not clear.
- I was confused by . . .
- I think the most interesting part was . . .
- I wonder why . . .
- I just thought of . . .

After some time working her way through the learning process, your child's metacognitive thoughts should evolve into more positive feelings like the following:

- I am not confused, I feel relaxed, I am in control of what I learn.
- I have enough information.
- I am confident in my ability to understand this subject.
- I can solve problems within this area or subject.
- I know I know how to learn new material.
- I am sure that I know how to learn this subject.
- I know what I have learned from this lesson that I can use later in life.

Note that while the comments are metacognitive (i.e., self-awareness), they also are emotional, with strong implications for perceived self-efficacy.

Table 4.1 gives a summary of learning strategies and examples of metacognitive questions applicable to each strategy.

COGNITIVE LEARNING STRATEGIES AND
THEIR CONCOMITANT METACOGNITIVE QUESTIONS

Along with self-awareness, there is the phenomenon of awareness of the minds of other children and other people in general. The child's developing mind goes through stages to arrive at what is sometimes called theory of mind, that is, the ability to recognize that what she thinks about something is not necessarily what others think or the ability to realize that each person has her own thoughts. At that point, metacognition begins to play a serious role in learning and thinking.

Before five years of age, the child does not yet possess a mental representational conception of the mind or, as I said above, does not recognize that others have their own thoughts.

THEORY OF MIND

A psychologist shows a five-year-old a candy box with pictures of candy on it and asks her what she thinks is in the box. "Candy," she says. Then the child looks inside and finds that the box contains crayons. The psychologist then asks her what some other child would think is in the box, and she replies "Candy" and chuckles at the deception.

Then the psychologist asks a three-year-old the same questions. The response to the first question is "Candy," as expected. But she is surprised to see the crayons, and when asked what another child would think is in the box, she answers "Crayons," and under further questioning, she goes on to say that she initially thought the box had crayons.

As a parent, reflect on your own development of awareness of what you know. At what age were you reasonably well able to identify what you do and do not know? Can you recall experiences when you had problems because you thought you knew something but actually did not? How do you feel about your knowledge now? Have you reached a point where you can seriously admit when you do not know something that maybe you should know?

Can you relate your own experiences with awareness to those of your children? Does that give you ideas about how to help them develop their own metacognition?

FIVE

Dispositions, Motivation, Attitudes: Desire to Think

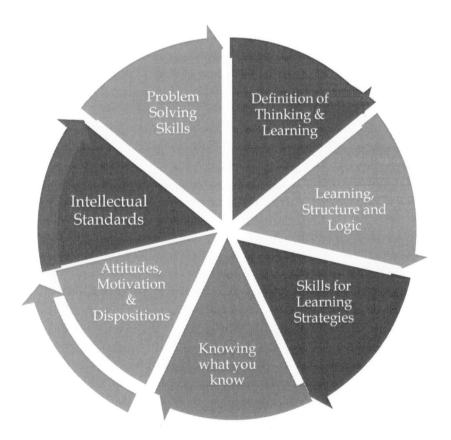

We have developed a logical chain of elements involving learning to think. In chapter 2, we explained how children learn and clarified the importance of learning in an organized and structured manner to facilitate further learning and to enable later recovery of what has been learned in order to apply it to problem solving. In chapter 3, we

explained in detail what cognitive strategies are and how to use them
to improve the efficiency and effectiveness of learning, to increase the
degree of structure of what is learned, and to facilitate recall and recovery of what was learned.

In chapter 4, we explained the role of metacognition—knowing what
you know and how you learned it. Solid awareness of what your child
knows, how it is being learned, and how the information is being stored
certainly expedites the whole process and leads to improved critical
thinking and problem solving.

Now we come to a critical issue: the motivation to learn and to think
critically. Knowing what is being learned and using cognitive strategies
and metacognition to facilitate and expedite learning are important and
useful. Yet the eagerness with which your child approaches learning
will be a function of his motivation, attitudes, and dispositions to learn.
These attitudes are not innate. They must be developed. Where are they
developed? In the home, by the family, by the extended family, and by
the church and related institutions.

Once your child starts school, teachers will also become involved in
motivation, but the lion's share of the effort must be done in the home
by parents. The motor that moves your child's learning is her motivation.
You as parents must start the motor and make sure you develop it.

We present the elements of motivation in the following fashion:

- Extrinsic motivation
- Interests
- Self-image
- Attribution of control
- Anxiety
- Emotional awareness

Then we discuss the basic dispositions, which are the following:

- Inquisitiveness
- Truth seeking
- Persistence
- Open-mindedness

Motivation and disposition are positions on a continuum. Motivation
is more immediate, more timely, and more opportune. Disposition is a
cumulative long-term tendency to perform and to be committed to performing in some way. We look first at affective factors in motivation and
then at dispositions.

Figure 5.1 shows the set of motivational factors and how they are related.

All six elements are emotional or affective. They have to do with how your child (or you) feels about his life, in general, and about learning and thinking in particular. These elements interact, as we will demonstrate.

EXTRINSIC MOTIVATION

Motivating your child to learn is important. There are two levels to the issue. The first is the matter of what we can call simply rewards and punishments. There is a relationship, sometimes called a "contingency," meaning that one event or stimulus or reward is dependent on another. An old friend of mine referred to this as "grandmother's rule," which was "First eat your peas, and then you can have some ice cream."

The basic idea is simple: Rewards and punishments can influence your child's behavior. And this is a powerful custom. Children respond well to rewards. If you offer a reward for some specific behavior, your child likely will respond in a positive manner. The contingency is "If you do this for me, I will give you something or do something for you or allow you to do something you wish to do."

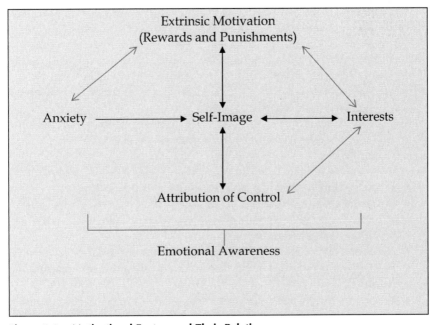

Figure 5.1. Motivational Factors and Their Relations

Direct contingencies are those arrangements we use to encourage our children (and ourselves) to do the daily things we should do but are not always so eager to do. If you say to your child, "First do your homework, and then you can watch television for 30 minutes," that is a direct contingency: Television (reward) is contingent on doing homework (the task). If your child asks for permission to go out to ride her bike, you can ask if the homework (or other relevant task) is finished and, if not, state the contingency: "First finish your homework, and then you may go to ride your bike."

My daughter Josephine and I arrange contingencies in relation to practicing the piano. She has preferences (like swimming, playing with her friends, playing on the computer or iPad, and so on), and they are made dependent on piano practice. She has internalized this type of arrangement, sees it as logical, and almost never complains about the contingency. The arrangement also contributes to the development of a positive disposition.

Many modern parents do not arrange the order of events in the proper manner but rather allow their children to engage in the more preferred activity first prior to performing the less desired activity, such as doing homework or household chores. This has the effect of depriving the child of learning the logic of contingencies, which are a fundamental part of real-world phenomena. It also often means leaving homework or other important tasks until the last minute when the child is tired and unenthused. Further, it fails to contribute to the development of positive dispositions.

Personal reinforcement history is the cumulative sum of what kinds of rewards and punishments we have had in the past and how they affect our current behavior. If your child has reacted well to rewards in the past, she will have developed a tendency to continue to react well to rewards. If she has not responded so well to rewards but has reacted better to intrinsic benefits, that will also predict what you as a parent should use to motivate her on a daily basis.

To teach your child how to develop self-monitoring of motivation and progress, it is useful to show her little actions she can take to help, such as the following:

- Set a deadline, a point at which the task should be done.
- Communicate the deadline to others (which increases the sense of duty).
- Break the task into parts.
- Select an easy part of the task to help her get started.
- Teach her to reward herself after each significant part is completed ("I did it!").
- Teach her to remove herself from distraction and get into an environment that facilitates study (turn off the television, find a quiet place, and so on).

Your child will have achieved her objective and developed a new pattern of behavior when she can work on a task until it is finished, even when she has trouble and cannot easily find an answer. You should provide constant supervision of her contingencies until she begins, bit by bit, to control them herself, which she *will* do.

INTERESTS

The second part of overt motivation is your child's interests, which are powerful motivators but are often difficult to develop. Many interests are simply part of a child's life. Eating, drinking soda, playing on the playground, and spending time with mom and dad are common interests among children. Unfortunately, some negative stimuli also are interesting, such as watching television, eating too many snacks, playing video games, chattering on the phone, and so on. Developing positive, useful interests requires time and attention, such as the following:

- Reading a book or story to your child each night as part of the going-to-bed routine
- Getting your child to listen to good music
- Watching quality, age-appropriate television programs and movies
- Looking at educational pages on the Internet
- Avoiding time wasters, such as video games

A first step as a parent is to identify the things your child likes to do and those she does not like to do. Those things are the beginning of interests. Then you should think seriously about what interests you would like to stimulate in your child. Do you want her to have a love of learning? Are you eager for her to take an interest in specific subjects, such as math, literature, or languages? Do you want her to develop strong spiritual feelings or a solid interest in good music? Are there sports activities you think should interest your child? Religious activities?

Encourage your child to talk about what she likes and dislikes. Watch her as she copies your behavior and your likes and dislikes as they become part of hers. Have you asked her what she likes? Does she like dinosaurs, animals, dolls, clothes, princess stories, ballet, music, swimming, or bike riding? Ask things such as the following:

- What do you want to be when you grow up?
- If you could live anywhere in the world, where would it be?
- Is reading important to you?
- Do you like reading by yourself?

- What kind of games do you like to play?
- Do you have a hero or a favorite person?
- Who are your best friends?

Exposure, mimicry, and sharing are three of the strongest ways to develop interests. Most little girls develop interest in clothes, particularly if their mothers are better-than-average or even fastidious dressers. If Mom likes Sudoku, her daughter will be inclined that way. If Dad plays chess, both son and daughter will develop at least a good bit of curiosity. The parents' choice of music will undoubtedly influence the child's interests.

This is an important kind of learning, called modeling, or vicarious learning. It is learning by watching others, seeing what they do, seeing when they succeed, seeing the benefits they gain, or seeing when they fail and the costs they pay. Your child will always be observing both parents, siblings, friends, and prestige figures (e.g., grandparents) and will constantly be learning in very subtle ways. You can support this observational learning by subtle encouragement:

- "Don't you just love this music?"
- "I really enjoy reading a good book."
- "When the family likes something I have cooked, I feel so good."

In relation to both extrinsic motivation and general interests, parents can help their children by delivering effective praise:

- Communicate contingently; that is, give praise when the task has been completed (not before or during).
- Be specific about what accomplishment is being praised: "You did that so well!"
- Give praise spontaneously to show that you are paying attention to what your child does.
- Use praise to provide information about the value of your child's accomplishments: "That is good; knowing how to divide is important!"
- Use praise to increase your child's sense of self-effectiveness: "See, you could do it!"
- Use praise to highlight noteworthy efforts by your child (when appropriate).
- Make sure that praise attributes success to effort and ability, implying that similar success can be expected in the future: "When you try hard, you always succeed!"
- Use praise to focus your child's attention on his own task-relevant behavior.

SELF-IMAGE

As a basic aspect of learning, you and your child develop opinions about yourselves in relation to learning. You are constantly developing, elaborating, and modifying your opinions about yourself in a wide range of situations. Here we are concentrating on your image in terms of learning and thinking. Self-image is the child (or any person) trying to answer the question "Who am I?" Most of that answer comes directly from the child's relations with her parents and family. The image a child has of herself is very much a matter of how she has been treated by the family.

If the family has always been primarily supportive and loving, your child most likely will have a positive image of herself. If the family has been too strict or too absent (father and mother working and with limited time at home), the child's image of self may be less strong and may be complicated or diminished.

Of all the thoughts that affect human functioning, the most important are self-efficacy beliefs, which are a person's judgment of his capabilities to organize and execute courses of action that will lead to desired types of performances. Self-efficacy beliefs touch every aspect of people's lives, whether they think productively or self-debilitatingly or optimistically or pessimistically.

Your child's self-image in relation to learning will be a combination mostly of your support and her success. Many educators and psychologists have proposed that if parents help their child develop a positive self-image, the child will then be an effective learner. That approach fails to comprehend that a good self-image actually comes from being able to do things.

Parents should help their children be successful at many things—reading, writing, math, dancing, playing the piano or violin, baseball, football, basketball, or chess—and in the process praise the children for their *accomplishments*. The joy that children feel when they can successfully perform is a major reward for them, and the recognition and praise of their parents is almost as strong a reward. Together, they are powerful. They motivate.

For many years, the self-esteem movement seemed to tell children that they were inherently valuable, which is true but not enough. Being told that you are great and learning to think that you are great does not replace being competent:

> Some children are victims of the self-esteem movement. They have a wholly unearned self-respect. No, an unearned admiration for themselves. And they've been given this high sense of themselves by parents and teachers who didn't and don't have time for them, and who make it up to them by making them conceited. I'm not sure how this will play out as they hit adulthood.
>
> What will happen to them when the world stops telling them what they have been told every day for the first quarter century of their lives, which is: You are wonderful. I always want to tell them: the only kind of self-respect that lasts is the kind you earn by honestly coming through and achieving. That's the only way you'll make a lasting good impression on yourself.[1]

The scientific term is "self-efficacy"—the "I-know-I-can" psychological phenomenon that enhances goal achievement. Self-efficacy isn't about a sense of self-worth; it's about believing that you are capable of producing a desired result—that you can achieve your goals. The truth is that there's so much more to "I think/know I can" than childhood fiction or a clichéd, feel-good maxim. Everyone has something they would like to change or improve; everyone has goals. Therefore, self-efficacy is of universal appeal and widespread need. Beyond that, it offers up some great benefits for potential adopters.

For example, people high in self-efficacy take better care of themselves, see tasks not as drudgery but as something to be mastered, and feel more empowered. They're not controlled by circumstances. They see setbacks as challenges to be overcome and can cope with hardship better than those with low self-efficacy. They learn from failure and channel it into success, like Thomas Jefferson, Walt Disney, and J. K. Rowling. People higher in self-efficacy also have a greater sense of motivation and persistence.

Perhaps most important, self-efficacy affects how we feel, think, and act. Low self-efficacy has been linked to helplessness, anxiety, and depression. Fortunately, whether your child's current level is average, ample, or absent, much like physical attributes, self-efficacy can be enhanced.

The concept of self-efficacy has generated research in areas such as medicine, athletics, business, social and political change, psychology, and education. In psychology, it has been the focus of studies on clinical problems (phobias, depression, assertiveness, and so on). Self-efficacy has been especially prominent in studies of educational constructs, such as academic achievement, attributions of success and failure, goal setting, social comparisons, memory, problem solving, and teaching and teacher education.

Researchers have established that self-efficacy beliefs and behavior changes and outcomes are highly correlated and that self-efficacy is an excellent predictor of behavior. In fact, self-efficacy has proven to be a more consistent predictor of behavioral outcomes than any other motivational construct. It is not simply a matter of how capable one is but also a matter of how capable one believes oneself to be.

There are some basic rules that parents can use to stimulate high self-efficacy in their children. The first rule is to *model* effective behavior. Your child watches everything you do. If she sees you as an effective and secure person, she will begin to integrate images and ideas of effectiveness. If she sees that you are persistent and almost always complete your various duties, whatever they may be, she will begin to internalize that behavior. If she sees that you procrastinate, she will learn that quite quickly.

The second rule is more concrete:

- Set reasonable expectations for your child and assign tasks and responsibilities that are within her existing capabilities but that at the same time create a small challenge.
- Monitor and assist your child to achieve the tasks.
- Provide feedback on the degree of effectiveness.
- Provide a reasonable amount of praise and perhaps rewards for successful completion.

A third suggestion is to use the concept of metacognition directly in relation to self-esteem. For example, ask your child the following:

- What has your teacher told you that you do well?
- What have your friends told you that you do well?
- What have your other adults told you that you do well?
- What do you enjoy doing because you know you do it well?

By stimulating awareness, you can help your child direct her energies toward the areas in which she can best develop her sense of self-effectiveness.

ANXIETY AND STRESS MANAGEMENT

Life is full of moments of anxiety and stress for all of us. As you attempt to teach your child to think well, stress and anxiety will occur. For example, if you push your child too hard to learn something new or to solve a new problem, he may feel stress or anxiety. He wants to live up to your expectations and worries that he will not and that you might love him less. The predicament is that your child is using short-term, or working, memory to solve the problem, and working memory is limited in the amount of substance it can store. If anxiety occurs, it takes up space in working memory that could be used to find strategies to solve the problem.

Think about your own experiences. If you are employed and must go to work on a day when your child has a cold or a mild fever and is going to school to take an important test, you will be worried about that situation much of the day, and those worries will use up some space in your working memory, perhaps reducing your effectiveness at work. The same thing happens when your child feels under pressure to do something. The pressure creates anxiety, which occupies a part of the memory that could be used to find solutions to the problems the child wishes to solve.

At a deeper level, anxiety is a main cause of motivation. Piaget referred to it as disequilibrium, as have some biologists. Evolutionary psychologists highlight the importance of survival anxiety as a major cause of human evolution: The ones who worried tended to be those who survived.

So anxiety is important. What is prejudicial is excessive anxiety, which is easy to understand but difficult to measure because each person responds to anxiety in her own way. You probably know a few people who seem to never show signs of anxiety (the "Clint Eastwood" of the group) and others who fall apart at the slightest bit of pressure.

Your child (or other children you know, such as your child's classmates) may suffer from anxieties related to learning and testing. It is typical to hear them say things like the following:

- I worry about the possibility of having to repeat the year.
- My worries about doing badly interfere with my concentration when I take tests.
- I get depressed when I get bad grades.
- I am easily distracted when I try to study—cell phone, television, and other things.
- I am not able to concentrate well when I am nervous, in a bad mood, or depressed.
- I get very scared and nervous when I have to take important tests.

In highly competitive societies, these worries lead to sickness and even suicide.

It seems clear that you would like to have your child be reasonably sensitive to her environment but also be able to cope easily with minor or even major stress. How do you achieve that? The first thing is to not overly shelter your child from stress.

The second thing is to verbally moderate situations of anxiety, somewhat like *The Little Engine That Could*, in the sense of telling your child that you are sure that he will be able to achieve what he wants if he makes an effort to do so. "I know you can do it if you try." Also, if he is showing signs of stress, calming language is useful. "Relax a little, be calm, breathe deeply, and then you can try again, and I am sure you can do it."

ATTRIBUTION OF CONTROL

All of us go through life trying to figure out why things happen. Sometimes we take responsibility for what happens, and sometimes we blame others. A typical example of this is grades on tests in school. Your child comes home with a good grade and says, "I got an A on the test!" She comes home with a bad grade and says, "The teacher gave me a D on the test." She claims responsibility when it is a good outcome and blames the teacher when it is a bad outcome.

How people attribute cause and responsibility is a function of four basic factors. The first is *ability*, real or perceived. The second is *effort*, that is, how much effort the child invests in the task. The third is *task difficulty*. Is the task challenging or easy? The fourth factor is chance or *luck*, which influences how a student perceives responsibility. If a child thinks he got lucky, he will not attribute the results to his own efforts.

Two students get an A on a test. The first one says, "Well it was easy, and I got lucky." The second one says, "I tried hard, and with my ability, I got a good grade." The first student assigns responsibility for his grade to luck and a low level of difficulty. The second student attributes his results to his effort and his ability. The first has what is called an external locus of control. He assigns the results to factors outside himself. The second student has an internal locus of control, meaning that he assigns responsibility for his results to elements under his control.

Which student would you want your child to be?

As a parent, you can have a major influence on your child's development of attribution. The practice is clear. Emphasize your child's efforts and ability and avoid attribution to external factors. If your child tells you he got lucky, correct him and tell him that his result came from his efforts. Among things you can do are the following:

- Make sure that assignments (tasks, tests, and so on) that you give him are challenging: not easy but also not too difficult.
- Encourage your child to understand that it is his personal effort that leads to success and always reward strong efforts and persistence.
- Encourage your child to realize that he has sufficient ability and talent to achieve his academic goals: "You can do it!"

The issue of attribution is important. Each child needs to develop a sense of responsibility for what she does and an ability to know when results are to her credit and when they are to her blame. It is a fundamental role of parents to ensure that this sense of responsibility is developed. This can be done by ensuring that your child understands the concept of personal responsibility. This means making sure that you always make her aware of what she is doing and the results of her actions. It is part of self-efficacy.

The kind of questions parents should ask here include the following:

- Did you really try hard?
- Are you sure you gave it all the effort you had?
- Did you study enough before the test?
- Why do you think the teacher gave you a bad grade?
- Did you break that toy?
- Are you being honest with yourself?

AFFECTIVE AWARENESS

You not only know what you know but also should know how you feel about what you know, how you feel about learning, how you react to teachers and others (boss, wife, friends, and so on), how you motivate yourself, and how you assume responsibility, among other issues. And you should think about these concepts because you will want to teach and stimulate them in your children. A group of emotional or affective factors are involved in living and learning. The emotional world of each individual and of groups, such as family and close friends, is a complex mixture of elements.

To effectively help your child to achieve her full potential, it is critical to understand how your child processes and interprets her interaction with the world around her. Your child is an active agent who is engaged in her own development and can make things happen through her actions. These actions will be guided primarily by emotional variables and how these variables develop and impinge on your child.

Young children often have limited awareness of their own emotions and are not able to reflect on them. As a parent, you should try to get your child to recognize and talk about his emotions. Start by asking questions such as the following:

- How are you feeling today?
- Were you happy with the grade you got on your test?
- Did you get scared when you saw that big dog barking?
- Do you enjoy playing with your classmates?

When your child talks, draw her out, ask more questions, and keep the questions focused on feelings: positive and negative. Try to help her understand her negative feelings. But the most important thing is to simply encourage her to talk about her feelings—to be aware of how she feels and how she reacts.

To review, take another look at figure 5.1. You may see that anxiety is the emotion that drives and influences the others. Anxiety affects how your child will respond to rewards. If she is too anxious, she will exaggerate the importance of the rewards. Anxiety will touch on the development of her self-image. If she is too anxious, her self-image will develop slowly. The same situation occurs with attribution of control. A highly anxious child will be more inclined to blame others and avoid responsibility.

Further, self-image will influence your child's interests, but her interests will also influence her self-image. If she gets good at something, such as math, dancing, or reading, she will be more interested in it and will have a better self-image in relation to it.

As your child develops a stronger sense of internal control and responsibility, her self-image will improve, and her reliance on external rewards will decrease—because she is internalizing responsibility. And that internalization will lead to the development of positive dispositions.

DISPOSITIONS TO LEARN, THINK, AND PERSEVERE

The review of emotions leads to the examination of the broader topic of attitudes and predispositions. These two concepts are similar. The first suggests a mental state or evaluation of some concept, person, event, or process. We say that she had a positive attitude toward studying. The second concept goes a bit further and suggests a deeper inclination, a tendency to act in a certain manner under given circumstances. The difference is subtle but important.

For example, I have a positive attitude about cinema; I like movies. But I do not go very often. My disposition is weaker than my attitude. Often children have a positive disposition toward learning but a weaker attitude toward studying. In the case of helping your children learn to think critically, as parents you will want to help them develop both a positive attitude and a positive disposition toward thinking.

In everyday parlance, we say things like the following:

- He had a dog with an excellent *disposition*.
- Her *disposition* was to always think negatively.
- He has a *disposition* toward criminal behavior.
- Her easy *disposition* and sociability masked the intensity of her feelings.

There are many examples of children who have the skills or the potential for developing the skills of thinking but who lack consistent internal motivation to use those skills. We all know people who are very intelligent and often well educated but who do not have the sufficient disposition to use their intelligence and their education to optimal effect. And many parents worry about how to help their children develop the kind of motivation that will help lead them to be successful thinkers and successful people.

A person's basic way of thinking is closely related to his basic way of being, of interpreting and responding to reality. The development of higher-order critical thinking and learning requires positive dispositions toward analytic and evaluative thinking.

One of the first steps for parents is to have a clear idea of what is required. The typical word is *disposition*, which is a customary mood and attitude toward the life around one, such as "a cheerful disposition." Related is the idea of *temperament*, which implies a pattern of innate characteristics associated with one's specific physical and nervous organization, such as "an artistic temperament." We use the concept of *temper* to refer to those qualities acquired through experience that determine how a person meets difficulties or handles situations, as in "a resilient temper."

Character is the term we use for the aggregate of moral qualities by which a person is judged apart from intelligence, competence, or special talents. Character is the development of a strong sense of right and wrong that can guide a child or adolescent (and then an adult) to make the correct decisions beneficial to a full and successful life. Character is also a major aspect of the sense of self, the feeling of internal consistency of one's behavior and beliefs.

For parents, character development is the deliberate effort to build and develop virtues that are good for the individual and good for society. Character as virtue affirms human dignity, promotes the well-being and happiness of the individual, serves the common good, and defines our rights and obligations. Religious upbringing is closely related to character development in all religions.

The concept of *personality* is oriented toward openness to new experiences, awareness of others, social and emotional competence, being outgoing, and, for teenagers (and many adults), being popular and well liked. Personality traits are individual and subjective and vary widely. Personality includes your sense of humor (or lack thereof), whether you're outgoing or shy or friendly or stoic, your interests, your passions, and so on.

While some people have well-developed personalities, their character sometimes is weak, and you eventually avoid them even though "they're a lot of fun." Some people will like any particular personality, while others are more discerning.

Character is inner directed. It has to do with knowing what is right and what is wrong. It has much to do with conformity, with learning and abiding by the values of the family, the clan, the community, and even the nation. It typically involves responsibility, respect, perseverance, honesty, and patriotism. Character traits are objective, constant, and timeless. Character traits include honesty, trust, respect, responsibility, leadership, loyalty, and courage. One's character can be objectively judged.

A strong, solid character is a tremendous asset that will increase your child's possibilities of long-term success. Character can be taught. However, educators are bypassing the difficulty of teaching character and have gone directly to self-esteem, the reward of strong character. But without character, self-esteem is a hollow, free-floating concept.

At its highest level, it is integrity, a firm adherence to a code of moral values, being honest, trustworthy, and incorruptible. Integrity should always be the highest goal one has for oneself and one's children. As Shakespeare said, "This above all: to thine own self be true, And it must follow, as the night the day, Thou canst not then be false to any man." Few politicians learn this lesson.

Personality is outer directed, relating to exterior situations, being open to new ideas, and willing to try new things. One of the principal complications of the lives of teenagers is a strong desire to be accepted by others—to be popular and to be liked. As teens experience strong cognitive and physical changes, they often begin to think of their friends and peer group as more important than their family. Because of peer pressure, they often indulge in behaviors that are inconsistent with their values and those of their family.

As they search for their own unique identity, adolescents frequently are confused about what is right and what is wrong. While generally positive, personality stress can lead to trying things that could be inconsistent with character (such as cheating, alcohol, drugs, and promiscuity). It also can and often does lead to antischool, antistudying biases in surroundings where it is bad to be thought of as a "nerd," as can be seen in many urban school systems.

The crucial dimension in all this development is conformity versus defiance. Development of character requires acceptance of and conformity to the values of the family (including religion). Obtaining a distinct personality means being able to defy some norms in search of one's own individuality.

If parents place too much emphasis on conformity, the teen may not develop a real individuality (e.g., as might happen in the Middle East or in India). But if parents do not insist on basic levels of conformity (i.e., they are too permissive), then aberrations develop, integrity is weakened, and popularity becomes more important (as often happens in societies like England and the United States).

Knowing when to accept or tolerate defiance in a child is one of the most important but also one of the most difficult tasks a parent faces. Simplified, the defiance is easier to accept when it is related to less important values than when it confronts fundamental values: A white lie is more tolerable than a blatant distortion of a basic truth. Knowing when to allow a child to do something the way he wishes instead of the way the parents would prefer is complicated but important. Yet parents should never forget the crucial formative nature of their role.

I remember once when my son was about three, and he wanted to do something I told him he could not. He said, "If you don't let me you won't be my friend." I said, "I am not your friend: I am your father."

In the case of my son, I was strict with him for most of his life. And I worried a lot about stunting his personality. As a young adult, he once told me, "You were very strict with me, so I learned to be strict with myself." He is a successful businessman, is happily married, and has no apparent vices (except golf!).

So as parents, you should stress character development over personality but try to figure out when to accept and permit defiance. For your child's good and for your own, you should not accept too much defiance because that will damage your child's respect for you and also will debilitate the full development of her self-esteem, self-respect, and integrity.

Dispositions can be learned, but they are subtle and difficult. Dispositions come from family influence but also from deep-seated, subconscious psychological influences. The big point is that parents and the immediate family have a tremendous influence on the development of a child's dispositions. The family, not school (which simply makes a weak attempt to develop attitudes), is crucial.

The dispositions that are required in the development of solid, critical, and creative thinking include the following:

- Inquisitiveness
- Truth seeking
- Persistence
- Open-mindedness

INQUISITIVENESS: CURIOSITY

The important thing is to not stop questioning. Curiosity has its own reason for existing. *Never lose a holy curiosity.*

—Albert Einstein, May 2, 1955

Inquisitiveness is an attitude closely related to curiosity. In its best sense, it means an attitude of examination or investigation, one given to asking many questions. Curiosity connotes an active desire to learn or to know. Many children are curious about everything. Inquisitiveness sometimes suggests habitual curiosity and persistent quizzing and under some circumstances may imply impertinence. In the sense that I am using the words here, it is to denote a positive curiosity leading to a more logical and scientific interest in a subject.

Some psychologists have suggested that curiosity and inquisitiveness are closely related to intelligence, which may have some truth to it. The great behaviorist Skinner said, "No one doubts the natural, innate curiosity of a child."

Curiosity is the most critical element for the mental development of your child. It helps your child clarify numerous problems. It helps develop new ideas and expressions, helps solve riddles and problems, and subsequently helps the child apply them in her daily life. Curiosity helps your child explore new and changing situations in her life. Asking questions and investigating diverse possibilities will help your child grow to be more inventive and creative. Stimulating curiosity helps your child enlarge her brain through the production of dopamine, which induces a sense of satisfaction.

Children naturally are curious, as I mentioned, but they often need help to develop it further. We had our first look at the role of questions in chapter 3. Questions are the most critical method for developing and stimulating curiosity. By asking questions, not only does the child learn, but her mind is most active, and she becomes more observant of the world around her. As new ideas occur, she expects and anticipates even more ideas that then are assimilated and accommodated in her mind.

Inquisitiveness is often accompanied by a related disposition that may be called systematicity or analyticity, which means an inclination toward reason and evidence to address problems and anticipate the consequences of events and ideas. People with a positive inclination toward systematicity favor approaching problems in an orderly and focused way.

For example, I am reasonably sure that I learned systematicity in school, not overnight and not because of overt actions by my teachers, possibly even as a rejection of things my teachers said and did. It was a long process that led me to become a strong proponent of the order and logic required by a systematic approach to problems. People who are high in this disposition tend also to have positive self-confidence about their reasoning abilities. This disposition also is closely related to truth seeking.

The opposite of inquisitiveness is indifference. Unfortunately, we see many children who are indifferent to the world around them. The main cause of their indifference is the lack of adequate attention from their parents and family, the failure to develop a sense of personal mastery and autonomy. Poverty and lack of education are also major contributors.

Knowing the importance of curiosity, here are some tips on how to develop it.

As a parent, you must keep an open mind and be open to learn, un-learn, and relearn. Some things you know and believe might be wrong, and you should be prepared to accept this possibility and change your mind. If your child has the impression that you are not open, she will naturally assume that openness is not important. This is essential if you are to have a curious mind. Remember, your child will model your behavior.

Teach your child to not take things for granted but to doubt reasons and to look at alternatives. If your child simply accepts the world as it is without trying to dig deeper, she will certainly lose curiosity. And as her parent, you should lead the way. Try to dig deeper beneath the surface of what is around you. A sure way to dig deeper is to ask questions:

- *What* is that?
- *Why* is it made that way?
- *When* was it made?
- *Who* invented it?
- *Where* does it come from?
- *How* does it work?

What, why, when, who, where, and *how* are the best friends of curious people.

Never label something as boring. Do not allow yourself to be bored. Be active. Search for interesting things to do. Whenever you label something as boring, you close one more door on possibilities. Curious people are unlikely to call something boring. Instead, they always see it as an entry to an exciting new world. Even if they don't yet have time to explore it, they will leave the door open to be visited another time.

Make learning interesting, even fun. If you or your child view learning as a burden, there's no way she will want to dig deeper into anything. That will just make the burden heavier. But if you think of learning as something fun, you will naturally *want* to dig deeper. So look at life through the glasses of fun and excitement and enjoy the learning process.

Be diverse in reading, in viewing, and in listening. Don't spend too much time on just one world; take a look at other worlds. That will introduce you and your child to the possibilities and excitement of other worlds, sparking your interest to explore them further. One easy way to do this is through reading diverse kinds of magazines and books. Pick a book or magazine on a new subject and let it feed your mind with the excitement of a new world. Another way is to find pages on the Internet that lead to interesting places, ideas, and images.

Limit the amount of television your child watches and pay careful attention to contents. Idle cartoons are not the same as *Little Einsteins, Imagination Movers,* or *Dora the Explorer.* Two hours a day should be the maximum.

Keep your child away from violent video games: They do almost nothing to help a child think, and they tend to develop antithinking habits. Also, they often stimulate hostility, aggression, and antisocial attitudes. (Some video games are positive but have to be chosen carefully.)

TRUTH SEEKING

As a disposition, this means simply to prefer the truth to falsehood or delusion and to dedicate oneself to search for the truth in just about all matters.

There is a concrete reality. The universe functions in certain ways and not others (try ignoring gravity or the other laws of physics). Truth is human understanding that is in accord with reality, with what actually is and occurs. Understanding that is absent (ignorance) and that is not in accord with reality (delusion) creates all sorts of problems in our lives. Analysis that is not based on truth misleads us, and action that is not based on truth goes awry. A high-quality life, a life that functions smoothly, is a life based on understanding the way things are and the way things work.

Do we want to know the truth about ourselves? About the world around us? About our place in the cosmos? Of course, but it is not always easy. Sometimes believing in delusions is easier and more comfortable. How many people read their horoscope or try homeopathic medicines?

Also, there is a question of the degree to which reality can be known. Three infamous French philosophers created a trend called postmodernism, which suggested that a concrete reality exists only to the degree that it is perceived and that perceptions can vary. That is called solipsism. Stay away from that silliness. The vast majority of the universes that exist through the process of cosmological evolution exhibit laws that are invariant under a wide range of significant transformations. Evolutionary cosmology gives us objective worlds.[2] Or, as we said above, there is a concrete reality.

The opposite of truth seeking is intellectual dishonesty, lack of rigor, and lack of desire to do the best and find the facts, certainty, and sureness. Postmodern relativism is a form of dishonesty. Modern politics are a major form of dishonesty. Political correctness is an attempt to subvert reality.

On a simpler level, as I write this, there is a spate of articles going around the Internet discussing the problems of cheating and plagiarism among high school and university students in several countries. Most of the articles say that pressure to perform, plus laziness and the availability of sources on the Internet, has led to a lowering of standards about honesty. That sounds like a big excuse. Cheating is untruth. Truth seeking and honesty must be cultivated.

PERSISTENCE OR PERSEVERANCE

As a disposition, persistence or perseverance means to persist in a state, enterprise, or undertaking in spite of counterinfluences, opposition, or discouragement. When the going gets tough, the tough get going. The basis of persistence is motivation.

Henry Ford said, "Whether you think that you can or you can't, you're usually right." Think about that statement. It is true.

Remember *The Little Engine That Could*?[3] The engine had to take his train over a high mountain. Defying impossible odds, the little engine did. But did we somehow miss the message of this tale? Fifty years have passed since the book was first published, and when trying to overcome hardship or pursue our dreams, many of us still think, "I can't." Sound familiar?

American President Calvin Coolidge said this:

Nothing in the world can take the place of persistence.
Talent will not:
Genius will not;
Education will not.
Persistence and determination alone are omnipotent.

Coolidge may have been going too far. Talent, genius, and education are all useful, but without persistence, your child will not achieve her goals:

> I do not think there is any other quality so essential to success of any kind as the quality of perseverance. It overcomes almost everything, even nature.—John D. Rockefeller

> Defeat is simply a signal to press onward.—Helen Keller

> Perseverance is a positive, active characteristic. It is not idly, passively waiting and hoping for some good thing to happen. It gives us hope by helping us realize that the righteous suffer no failure except in giving up and no longer trying. We must never give up, regardless of temptations, frustrations, disappointments, or discouragements. —Joseph B. Wirthlin

> Our greatest weakness lies in giving up. The most certain way to succeed is always to try just one more time.—Thomas Alva Edison (It has been suggested that Edison tried more than 1,000 substances before settling on the carbon filament for his lightbulb.)

> That which we persist in doing becomes easy to do; not that the nature of the thing has changed, but that our power to do has increased.—Ralph Waldo Emerson

Examples abound. Walt Disney was turned down 302 times before he got financing for his dreams. Colonel Sanders spent two years driving across the United States looking for restaurants to buy his chicken recipe. He was turned down 1,009 times.

Abraham Lincoln is an exemplary case of persistence. The road to becoming perhaps the greatest president was a difficult one. As a young man, his family was forced out of their home. He had to work to support them. His mother died. A few years later, he failed at business. In his efforts to win a legislative position, he lost four times. He could not get into law school. He failed in business again. He was engaged to marry, but his fiancée died. He finally won a seat in Congress, did a good job, but then lost reelection. But he kept trying and, finally, in 1860, was elected president of the United States.

There is an aspect related to truth seeking and to persistence that is called compulsivity or compulsiveness, meaning feeling compelled to do something. Compulsion may be an irresistible persistent impulse to perform an act (as excessive hand washing, something that I do). Psychologists sometimes joke that if I am doing it, the act is persistence, while if you are doing it, it is compulsiveness. My daughter Josephine grows up with two compulsive, perfectionist parents. She already shows signs of perfectionism and compulsion. She will do great things (if she doesn't get too anxious and frustrated).

In all dispositions, encouragement and mentoring in the use of reflexive observation when undertaking a task or trying to solve a problem will increase your child's self-confidence and reduce self-doubt in his thinking and hence reduce errors. Engaging students in thoughtful and logical projects that require reflection will have positive effects on their thinking.

As a parent, the main contributions you can make to develop your children's persistence are the following:

- Inculcate, encourage, instill, and inspire your children to try and try again.
- Generously reward academic efforts both when successful and when they fail, emphasizing the importance of effort.
- Model persistence constantly and with accompanying commentary about the relation of effort and capability combined with determination: "See, it took me time, but I finished the job!"
- Encourage them to believe in their ability to carry out a plan.
- Teach them to develop organized plans toward the goals they wish to achieve.
- Show them that sympathy, understanding, and cooperation with others tend to develop persistence: "If we work on this together, we will make more progress."
- Encourage them to develop the habit of concentrating their thoughts on building of plans for the attainment of a definite purpose.
- Frequently remind them that persistence is the direct result of habit.

The subjects of motivation, interests, self-image, and attribution of control all contribute to dispositions, particularly to persistence. The main element that a parent should keep ever present is the emphasis on effort. Achievements should not be attributed to intelligence or to luck. Children should be taught that their personal effort is the most important feature of their achievement. Persistent hard work is the key to successful learning and subsequent success in life.

You will want your child to develop ideas such as the following:

- I am to be very good at whatever I do.
- Anything worth doing is worth doing right.
- To reach my goals, I may have to overcome setbacks.
- I must be a very hard worker to reach my goals.
- I will finish whatever I begin.
- Achieving something of significant importance is a high goal in my life.

OPEN-MINDEDNESS

To have an open mind means to be willing to consider or receive new and different ideas. It means being flexible and adaptive to new experiences and ideas. Combined with persistence, flexibility or open-mindedness creates the most powerful psychological dispositions necessary for success. In personality theory, openness is one of the four robust dimensions, where it is shared with intelligence, culture, and inquisitiveness. The opposite attitude or disposition is intolerance, narrow- or closed-mindedness, and prejudice.

Cultivating an open mind in your child is another valuable aspect of critical thinking. The world is growing more complex, knowledge and information are becoming more important in the domain of productivity, and technology is adding new tools, such as the Internet, mobile phones, and digital photography, making life more interesting.

People who are open-minded are willing to adjust their views when they receive new information, new facts, and new evidence. Therefore, they tend to be more rational, careful, and flexible. If your child is willing to look for new ways of doing and evaluating things, her intellectual life will expand and be more satisfying. Being open to new ideas also is a considerable help in problem solving because it increases the options we can consider.

People who are more open-minded tend to be more accepting of others, although open-mindedness does not preclude standards such as moral and religious values. If your son or daughter learns to be a little more open, he or she will also probably be a little more optimistic about life, suffer less stress, want to learn more, and have better problem-solving skills.

Keep in mind that there is always a tension between truth, curiosity, and open-mindedness. Persistence also at times clashes with open-mindedness, and too much open-mindedness implies lack of standards, so this is a good time to proceed to that subject.

Six

Developing and Establishing Intellectual Standards for Thinking

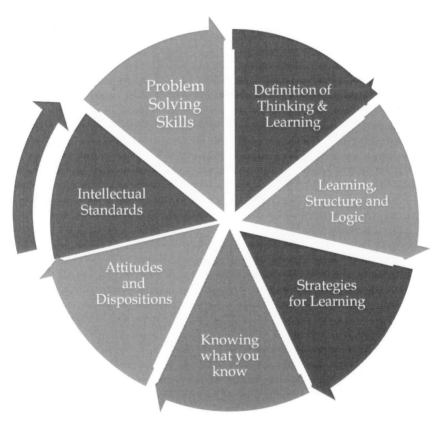

Once attitudes and dispositions have been approached, understood, and appreciated and are being inculcated and your child is learning through cognitive strategies and metacognition, it becomes time to look at the intellectual standards you will expect when she solves a problem, prepares an essay, answers questions about what is being learned, and so on. We can think of these standards as dispositions toward thinking and values, criteria, or principles about what is quality thinking. They are closely related to attitudes and dispositions because while these have to do with temperament toward thinking, standards establish the worth or value of what is being learned.

The general concept of standards should be clear but can often be confusing. In its basic form, standards are values or principles set up and established by authority as a rule for the measure of quantity, weight, extent, value, or quality. They are *criteria*, a word that comes from the Greek meaning "judging" or "deciding."

In the United States (and other countries), general standards are a hot topic and are currently conceived of as curricular issues, that is, statements of what information should be taught to students. The typical school approach is this: What content should the students learn?

> Educational standards define the knowledge and skills students should possess at critical points in their educational career. Standards serve as a basis of educational reform across the nation as educators and policy makers respond to the call for a clear definition of desired outcomes of schooling and a way to measure student success in terms of these outcomes. (From an official government document)

The desired learning outcomes are seen mostly as subject matter mastery, that is, what can be measured on tests, which, interestingly, are referred to as *standardized* tests. Again, the main emphasis is on content to be learned.

INTELLECTUAL STANDARDS

Another area where teaching is more intuitive than direct, more subtle than planned, and more presumed than assumed is that of intellectual standards. Dispositions are attitudes that your child can develop with your help and guidance. Intellectual standards are benchmarks against which you and your child can measure his progress. In your efforts to help your child learn to think critically, you will want to adopt standards that are directly related to the quality of thinking and the expression of the results. Here we propose using standards identified and developed by Paul and Elder.[1]

If you ask teachers what are their intellectual standards when they teach, most may make vague statements about the truth but probably not more than that. They were not usually taught about standards: They were taught content (subject matter) and how to deliver it to students.

Because of curricular actions over the past two decades, most teachers will think in terms of the content standards we mentioned above. If given a chance to learn about teaching thinking, most teachers express interest, but when they return to the classroom, they usually go back to teaching the same way they were taught: emphasis on content.

Good-quality thinking is the examination of suggestions that are offered for acceptance to find out if they adequately match reality. Critical thinking is a mental habit and a developed power. It is a safeguard against delusion, deception, and superstition. We all live in a world of thoughts. Some we accept as true or highly probable (like gravity), and others we reject as highly improbable, implausible, or false (like flying saucers).

The problem is that some of the thoughts we identify as true are sometimes false, unsound, or misleading. And sometimes the thoughts we identify as false and trivial are true and significant. By our nature as humans, we are subject to uncertainty in the form of the following:

- We misapprehend ourselves and our earthly circumstances.
- Our minds do not always naturally grasp the truth.
- We do not always naturally see things completely as they are.
- We do not always automatically know what is reasonable or unreasonable.
- We frequently see things as we want them to be, not as they are (confirmation bias).
- We unconsciously twist reality to fit our preconceived ideas.

In order to reduce errors and, particularly, in order to teach our children how they can reduce errors in thinking, we should take rational control of our thinking processes to help determine what to accept and what to reject and what to be dubious about or more willing to trust. That means that we (and our children) need standards, principles, and guidelines that direct us to consistently excellent thinking.

So what are such standards?

CLARITY

Clarity is the condition of being clear, lucid, sharp, and apparent. It is the opposite of cloudiness, opacity, or obscurity. This is a major standard: the biggest benchmark for your child to achieve. It means that what is said or written is easily understandable, can be grasped free of ambiguity, is not obscure or vague, is adequately elaborated, and can be expressed in different ways or illustrated through examples. When a child makes a statement at home or in class or answers a question, the response should be clear, and the concepts used should be appropriate.

Sounds good, but it is not easy, and it requires training and practice.

Development of clarity should begin early. While encouraging children to think and to speak up in the early years, the parent must also place emphasis on clarity in a guiding fashion and through the use of clear examples, modeling what are clear statements. In the early years, when children are just learning new concepts, precision can be given less emphasis, but as their command of basic concepts grows, their ability to make clear statements should also grow.

Parents should help their children develop clarity from five years on. This is done by two basic actions: pointing out when something is not clear and demonstrating how to make it more clear. The first step is easy but requires vigilance. Parents sometimes get so used to ambiguity in what their children say that they do not bring it to their children's attention. It may not be necessary or even possible to point out lack of clarity *every time*, but it should be done as often as possible. Just say the following:

- Excuse me, that was not very clear.
- Can you repeat that more clearly, please?
- What did you mean by ———?
- Would you say more about ———?
- Can you give an example of what you are talking about?
- That was vague. Can you restate it more clearly?
- What is the difference between ——— and ———?
- Can you be more explicit?
- If I understand, you mean ———. Is that right?
- Is the most important point ——— or ———?
- Do you know what that word means? Can you tell me using a different word?
- Would this be an example? Can you give another example?

ACCURACY

Accuracy means free from error, especially as the result of care, such as an *accurate* diagnosis. It means conforming exactly to truth or to a standard or being able to give an accurate result. For example, when you weigh yourself or when you take your blood pressure, you want the devices to give you answers that are free from error.

This standard means that what is presented does not contain errors, mistakes, or distortions. Thinking can be more or less accurate: Does it represent things as they really are? How can your child check to see if her ideas and thoughts and statements are true? How can parents teach our children to verify the alleged facts? Can we trust the accuracy of the information given and the source from which it comes?

Children tend to trust their parents implicitly, and this can lead them into inaccuracies if the parents are not reasonably strict about the accuracy of what they say. My father used to tease me to show issues of accuracy, like saying, "I've told you a million times to keep your room clean." The key questions for accuracy are the following:

- Can you be more specific?
- How many kids were in the park?
- Are you sure that number is correct?
- When did that happen? What date?
- Who said what to whom?
- Are you sure that is correct?

PRECISION

To be precise means to be exact to the necessary level of detail, to be specific. It requires exactitude, fineness, preciseness, rigor, and veracity. A statement can be clear and accurate but not precise (Jack is overweight). What do we mean by overweight? How does it differ from obesity? Thinking and speaking should be as precise as possible.

At the primary school level and at home, precision is taught first through spelling and math. The words your child learns must be spelled correctly and pronounced correctly. The math answers must be precise: Two plus two cannot be five.

Of course, there are times when precision is not necessary, as when one is creating tales or stories about events. There are occasions when exaggeration may be permitted.

But you will want to teach your child to discriminate when and how that is possible. In another great play on the concept of precision, Ralph Waldo Emerson said, "There is no one who does not exaggerate." So we have Voltaire and Emerson warning us of the high risk of exaggeration. The risk exists, but if you wish to teach quality standards to your child, you will help him to learn about the importance of precision, when it is necessary, and how to avoid exaggeration:

- Can you give me more details about that?
- Could you be more specific?
- Could you express your claims more fully?
- Have you exaggerated any aspect of your position?
- Have you used questions most relevant to your current situation?

Teach your child to answer with the core ideas and concepts first, then provide more details.

LOGIC

"Logic" . . . [is] . . . the name of a discipline which analyzes the meaning of the concepts common to all the sciences, and establishes the general laws governing the concepts.

—Alfred Tarski (1901–1983; from his *Introduction to Logic and to the Methodology of Deductive Sciences*, xi)

The fourth standard is logic; that is, do the parts and how they are arranged make sense, and do they make for sound judgment and reasoning? Thinking can vary in its degree of logic. And in a book about teaching children to think, the main point is to lead them to think in an orderly way that closely resembles reality and is "logical."

In chapter 2, we stressed the idea that all the information that your child learns, particularly in relation to some sort of sphere, will have a logical internal structure. In chapter 3, we suggested that the correct use of the various learning strategies would increase the development of a solid structure of knowledge that would be logical in the sense that all the pieces of knowledge would fit into place in an ordered and coherent manner.

So when we teach our children to be logical, we ask them if what they are saying or thinking is consistent and integrated. Does the whole thought or the components of the thought fit together sensibly and plausibly? Does the answer demonstrate the correct structure? Does it fit into a recognizable pattern? (Remember that the role of structure, logic, and patterns is to help understand the world around them.)

One of the main tests of logic to answer is whether what your child says follows from the evidence. Can your child identify and provide examples that help establish the veracity of what has been said?

And there is always the test of "does this really make sense?"

- Does the solution make sense?
- Do the pieces of the solution fit together tightly?
- What is the line of reasoning that brought you to this point?
- Can you explain the process you have used to come to this conclusion?
- Can you show how this answer fits into the overall structure of the domain?

When teaching logic, one basic domain is called informal logic. Formal logic is deductive analysis reasoning based on syllogisms that relate categories or conditions, affirming or denying certain circumstances. It applies to mathematics. Most other subjects use informal logic, which functions as the model for everyday logic, where the conclusions may contain new information that is not present in the premises but that can be asserted with confidence if the statements adhere to the conventions of informal reasoning.

It is also useful to teach your child to recognize threats to informal logic, which occur every day and cause confusion. Some of these are shown in table 6.1.

There are many other fallacious arguments that you may want to teach your children, such as the gambler's fallacy, the historian's fallacy, the fallacy of division, the fallacy of composition, the masked man fallacy, the circular cause and consequence, and so on. For more detail, see http://www.amap.org.uk/developing-arguments-teachers-pack/informal-logic and http://plato.stanford.edu/entries/logic-informal.

Clarity, precision, accuracy, and logic form a group of important standards; call them the "big four." They are the fundamental standards that children must learn. As a parent, you should pay close attention to them and encourage your children to develop respect for them. Also, you should be modeling these standards through your own behavior.

These standards do not mean that your child cannot have imaginary friends or tell stories or occasionally exaggerate, all of which relate to the development of their potential creativity. But they should have a strong grasp of the significance of these standards, and most of their learning behavior should be guided by the big four.

RELEVANCE

Something is relevant when it bears on or relates to the matter at hand. It is pertinent, appropriate, apt, and fit. Normally, we look for a close logical relationship with the matter under consideration. This is part of the development of the underlying structure of the subject at hand. When your child is responding to questions related to problems being solved, you will want her to give relevant responses. Her ability to do that depends to a significant degree on how well she learned the structure and purpose of learning, as explained in chapter 2.

There is an interaction between learning and the sense of relevance. If your child does not feel that the content is relevant during learning, then serious engagement is difficult. So it is the goal of the parent to make sure that what your child is learning is seen as relevant, pertinent, and coherent. Children will sometimes ask, "Why are we learning this? Why do I need to know this? Why are we spending so much time on this?"

When students don't see the connection between the content and activities of the course and their future lives, they question what's happening and what we ask them to do. Research confirms that perceived relevance is a critical factor in maintaining student interest and motivation.

Table 6.1.   Types of Fallacies

Type of Fallacy	Definition	Example
Appeal to emotion (*argument ad populum*)	The fallacy of attempting to win popular assent to a conclusion by arousing the feeling and enthusiasms of the multitude.	"But officer, I don't deserve a ticket; everyone goes this speed. If I went any slower, I wouldn't be going with the traffic."
Appeal to pity (*argument ad misericordiam*)	When pity or a related emotion, such as sympathy or compassion, is appealed to for the sake of getting a conclusion accepted.	Public schools should have much easier exams for students because teachers don't realize the emotional repercussions of sorrow and depression of the many students who could score much better on easier exams.
Appeal to force (*argumentum ad baculum*)	The fallacy committed when one appeals to force or the threat of force to bring about the acceptance of a conclusion.	"All those opposed to my arguments for the opening of a new department, signify by saying, 'I resign.'"
Appeal to authority (*argumentum ad verecundiam*	Appealing to the testimony of an authority outside his special field. Occasionally, this argument is called the "argument from prestige" based on the belief that prestigious people cannot be wrong.	The U.S. policy toward mainland China was surely mistaken because Shirley MacLaine, the well-known actress, had grave misgivings about it.
Red herring fallacy	A "red herring" is an answer, given in reply to a questioner that goes beyond an innocent logical irrelevance. A red herring is a *deliberate* attempt to divert a process of enquiry by changing the subject.	"I think that we should make the academic requirements stricter for students. I recommend that you support this because we are in a budget crisis and we do not want our salaries affected."
Appeal to ignorance (*argumentum ad ignoratiam*)	The fallacy that a proposition is true simply on the basis that it has not been proven false or that it is false simply because it has not been proven true.	One argues that God or telepathy, ghosts, or UFOs do not exist because their existence has not been proven beyond a shadow of doubt or vice versa.
Ad hominem argument	The fallacy of attacking the character or circumstances of an individual who is advancing an argument instead of trying to disprove the truth of the statement or the soundness of the argument.	Francis Bacon's philosophy should be dismissed since Bacon was removed from his chancellorship for dishonesty.
Guilt by association	Guilt by association is the attempt to discredit an idea based on disfavored people or groups.	Hitler was a vegetarian; therefore, vegetarianism is wrong.

When your child is asked to work on solving a problem, the relevance and coherence of original learning becomes apparent. If she can make relevant responses, that is evidence that during original learning, she was able to relate pieces of learning in an articulate structure.

Thinking is always capable of straying away from the task:

- How does this fact bear on the issue?
- How does this idea relate to this other idea?
- Can you explain how your example, statement, or story is connected to the current issue?
- How does your question relate to the issue?
- How can that idea or concept be applied in practice?
- Can your idea be related to an everyday application?
- How is it relevant? What is its relationship to the issue at hand?

SIGNIFICANCE

There is an obvious value in information in terms of "getting to the point," of finding the meaningfulness of the subject at hand. Significance means having importance, being of consequence, having substantial meaning (meaningfulness). Although many ideas may be relevant, they often are not equally important, so we want our children to be able to identify the most significant information they need to deal with a particular issue. They should be able to identify which of a given group of ideas is the most important, which of these questions is the most significant:

- Which of these ideas is the most decisive in formulating your answer?
- Which of these elements is the most essential?
- Does one of these components have more strategic importance than the others?
- Is that idea more prominent in the overall explanation?
- Is there an element in this explanation or solution that appears to be more crucial or distinctive than others?
- Is there an idea here that is exceptional or impressive in terms of the solution to the problem?
- What part of this idea most likely has great meaning or lasting effect?

Again, your child's ability to be able to recognize significance will have much to do with the circumstances of initial learning. The strategies of learning should have helped to create a structure where the importance of certain elements over others is reasonably clear.

DEPTH AND BREADTH

These are two closely related standards. They are often contrasted, suggesting that it is not possible to get both. For example, a typical comment about the primary and secondary curriculum in the United States (and several other countries) is that it is a mile wide (breadth) but only an inch deep (depth), meaning that it is very superficial. This accusation is probably true.

When we talk about depth of thinking, we mean that the person knows more than a little and has a more profound knowledge of the subject. In the case of literature, a person who has read 10 major works of classic literature has a good start but cannot be compared to a person who has read more than 100 works. Depth means containing complexities and multiple interrelationships, with thoroughness of thinking that probes beneath the surface, goes deeper, and asks if this question is simple or complex. Depth includes information: How well does the child know the subject? How much time and information has he acquired in relation to the subject?

Depth means complexity, thoroughness, an understanding of intricate details about a subject. It typically involves engaging students' imaginations and emotions in learning, and it builds confidence and pride in their knowledge. As we insisted in chapter 2, a good structure is one that is very well articulated and that is achieved by learning a great deal about a subject and its internal, underlying organization.

A child who has breadth but not depth has little chance of spontaneously developing depth anywhere. Having depth without breadth is a problem, too, but it is less common and usually less serious.

Some questions to stimulate depth as well as to ascertain your child's depth are the following:

- What makes this concept so complex?
- What are the components of the concept that must come together?
- Can you provide further details of the subject, idea, or concept?

In thinking, depth also means to use reasoning processes that are not superficial but that truly deal logically with the complexities inherent in the question.

Breadth of knowledge usually refers to the number of topics mastered by the child within a particular area, such as a subject (mathematics) or a period (nineteenth-century American history). *Comprehensive* is the word most associated with breadth, meaning wide ranging or embracing a broad perspective on a subject. Sometimes the idea of open-mindedness is also included because the broader the range of knowledge, the greater the tendency to develop more openness and flexibility of thinking. Lack of breadth is often associated with inflexibility, partiality of view, and more prejudiced thinking.

Questions that a parent may use to stimulate breadth include the following:

- What points of view are relevant to this issue?
- What are the different perspectives available to view this issue?
- Have you looked at opposing views in an objective manner?
- What is my ethical responsibility?

FAIRNESS

The final standard we will mention is fairness. We want our children to develop a strong sense of justice, a vision of impartiality, equity, and reasonableness. Their thinking should reflect justice, honesty, a dedication to objectivity and a respect for others, and tolerance and should be relatively free of favoritism (like the disposition toward truth seeking or that of integrity). This is not easy, as humans have a strong natural tendency to try to confirm what they already believe (confirmation bias). Questions to ask your child when she is thinking, particularly when making judgments, include the following:

- Is the manner in which you are addressing the problem fair?
- Are the concepts being used justifiably?
- Who has vested interest in these issues?
- What assumptions are made by the author of the book you are reading?
- Have you seriously tried to be impartial?
- Have you thought of the viewpoints of other people related to the subject?
- Have you considered that different cultures might have varying opinions on this subject?

SUMMARIZING INTELLECTUAL STANDARDS

Your child is learning to think critically. She has developed a general grasp of what it means to learn and with your help has learned cognitive learning strategies that notably increase the effectiveness and durability of learning.

She has learned to use mindfulness or metacognition to facilitate learning and problem solving and to help provide personal feedback on progress and adequacy of learning. You have paid attention to and have understood the importance of developing dispositions and managing her interactions with emotions. You know that self-efficacy is the key to motivation and successful learning and application.

You have seen how the learning and application of intellectual standards can increase the effectiveness and quality of learning and responding through recovery, transfer, problem solving, and creativity. You know that these standards can reduce your child's misapprehension of herself and her earthly circumstances and help her be aware that her mind does not always naturally grasp the truth but requires effort and benchmarks to do so.

She can use these standards to help see things fully as they are and better grasp what is reasonable or unreasonable and to help reduce the bias of twisting reality to serve her purpose and help her to see the world as it is, not as she might wish it was.

SEVEN

Problem-Solving Skills

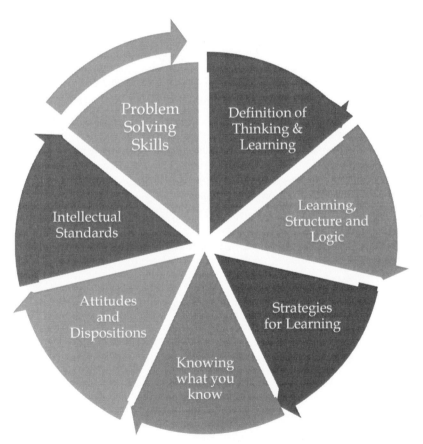

The primary reason we learn is to be able to use our learning for actions that are practical, pleasurable, and fruitful in our lives. We learn to appreciate music and art because they provide aesthetic pleasure to us. We learn to cook because it provides pleasant, tasty things to eat and to share with our families and others. We learn some subjects because they relate to our long-term career objectives. Often we learn other subjects and ideas (politics, history, psychology, literature, and so on) simply for the enjoyment of being knowledgeable.

Many other subjects we learn are meant to provide us with knowledge and skills that will allow us to perform in ways that improve our lives. That often means being able to think critically and solve problems.

When we have a problem to solve, we think critically. One does good critical thinking if one is facing challenges and solving problems. It is difficult to solve problems effectively unless one thinks critically about the nature of the problems and how to go about solving them. So critical thinking is working our way through a problem to a solution.

The top professions in the United States are also those that require the highest levels of critical thinking. These jobs are in the areas of medicine, pharmacy, law (particularly judges), information and computer systems, biological sciences, political science, and high-level business management.

In this book we have followed a logical line of development in teaching children to think critically. First, we looked at how they learn (constructing their knowledge), then at what they learn (units of knowledge that have an internal, logical structure). Then we examined in more detail how they learn—through developing cognitive strategies. That subject was followed by a discussion of the role and development of awareness of learning (i.e., metacognition) and the affective variables that influence learning and your child's general dispositions that set attitudes about learning.

Having set the stage, we then examined the quality controls—the intellectual standards that our children should learn to know, appreciate, and apply to make the value of their learning high in quality.

Now we have arrived at the action stage, the point where your child puts his learned knowledge to use in solving problems.

We look at two major aspects of problem solving. The first is the process or series of steps that lead to problem solving. What happens to make it possible to solve problems? Then we look at four different ways to solve problems and review the best ways to teach your children.

RESPONSE PRODUCTION STRATEGIES

"Response production strategies" is a fancy way to describe recovering the correct information or skills required for getting to the resolution of a problem. Three stages are involved.

First, your child has to recover the relevant knowledge and skills required for the problem or the situation at hand. Sometimes that is enough.

How much is 12 times 12? Who was the 14th president of the United States? It's like playing *Jeopardy!* Just knowing the answers to questions about information is good, is often useful, and can be much fun and satisfying. It is mini–problem solving.

Second, often your child then has to transfer or generalize the knowledge and skills to a new situation. What is learned in school and at home will be used in new situations mostly outside of school and home.

Finally, she has to apply a problem solving methodology in order to achieve her goal. There are a couple of seemingly natural methodologies, and there is one systematic methodology. Here we explain, describe, and analyze each.

RECOVERY—REMEMBERING

The first step is to ascertain if your child has the required knowledge in her long-term memory. What is the square root of 49? Who was the 34th president of the United States? What is the importance of the present continuous tense? State the implications of the Combined Law of Gases. Whatever the question, your child must delve into her long-term memory to find the required information. Remember that something is considered to be learned only if it is stored in long-term memory.

If I ask most American children what is 13 times 13, they probably will not have the response automatically available and will have to do mental calculations to answer the question. That is because in American schools, children typically memorize the multiplication tables up to 12 times 12. The use of calculation, either on paper or in the head, is a simple example of basic problem solving.

Successful recovery (remembering) is a direct result of how well the information was originally learned, including how well it is embedded into a structure. Random or isolated elements will be more difficult to remember than elements that are part of a structure. The structural relations also offer a clear path to how a parent can stimulate recall by asking your child to remember to what element the item is linked:

- Do you remember when you learned this? Was it in class or at home?
- Is this part of a bigger idea that you learned?
- How does this relate to other things you learned about this subject?
- Do you have an image or mnemonic for this item?
- Do you remember how you learned this?
- Was this part of a concept map you learned?
- Did you learn this through comparison and contrast?
- Is this part of an analogy or a metaphor?

In this stage, the critical role of priming and phrasing of cues/questions ("sounds like") is the best way parents can help their children recover stored knowledge.

SIMPLE APPLICATION

As mentioned in chapter 2, there are two levels of learning: One is the fundamental and important accumulation of information, basically facts and concrete subjects, and the other is the learning of concepts, rules, and principles that will allow your child to operate in and on the world. In the first level, she will be able to tell you the square root of 49 or what is 12 times 12. At the second level, she will be able to tell you the square root of 196 (which we presume she has not memorized) by applying the rules for determining square roots and by operating on her environment. She also will be able to calculate 16 times 16 by applying the appropriate rules. Further, she will be able to explain and apply abstract concepts, compare and contrast, and use logic to solve problems.

The ability to apply what has been learned is very important both for its practical effect—the correct answer—and for strengthening the underlying mental structure and assuring that your child builds confidence in his own abilities. Parents should also monitor responses to ensure that they are accurate and meet the intellectual standards established for good responses.

TRANSFER

Children learn things in relatively specific contexts, such as the home and the classroom. Then they should be able to use what they have learned in a broader context, such as at a higher level of education, in opportunities around the home or on the playground, and eventually in their daily lives. The main reason for formal schooling is to facilitate learning and acting in situations *outside* of school. Education should prepare students to function optimally in their future lives, so being able to transfer or generalize what they learn is a fundamental issue. Schools often seem to forget this point.

Simple generalization is the ability to use elements of stored knowledge under slightly different circumstances. Think of the following example. If you learned to drive in a small car, you should be able to drive other, similar small cars without much trouble. That would be close or near generalization; that is, the new task is very similar to the original situation. But if you have to drive a much bigger car, then the generalization (sometimes called transfer) is different and will require you to apply small-car knowledge and skills in a more challenging situation.

Imagine then that you must drive a large truck. You can envision that many things you learned in the small car can be transferred to the truck, but the size of the truck, its gears, its length, and so on may be so challenging that you cannot successfully generalize and master it.

We see this when students who have learned to add three-digit numbers to two-digit numbers can then add three-digit numbers to three-digit numbers and three-digit numbers to four-digit numbers:

Original learning

```
 345        452
+ 57       + 43
```

New learning: simple generalization

```
 427       5382       2853
+367       + 425      +3471
```

Much of math is simple progressive generalization. For example, in third-grade addition, there is a sequence that goes as follows:

- Add two numbers up to three digits
- Add three or more numbers up to three digits
- Add two numbers with four or more digits
- Add three or more numbers with four or more digits

Each step brings in a new element which builds on and generalizes previous learning. Of course this is also building and consolidating the addition scheme and the mathematics structure.

In fourth-grade multiplication, a typical sequence is the following:

- Multiplication to 12
- Multiply one-digit numbers by large numbers
- Multiply a two-digit number by a two-digit number
- Multiply a two-digit number by a larger number
- Multiply numbers ending in zero
- Multiply three numbers up to two digits each

As in the previous example, each step brings in a new element that builds on and generalizes previous learning. The path of generalization is clear.

We see simple transfer when a child learns to apply a rule, such as "*i* before *e* except after *c*." Having learned the rule, the child will be able to apply it to many words: *receive, conceive, conceivable, receivable,* and so on. She will simply have to remember the rule (which is a form of mnemonic).

Broader generalization or transfer occurs when your child can use stored information in different contexts. Suppose a child is given a problem like the following (see figure 7.1):

> A carpenter has 32 meters of lumber and wants to make a border around a garden bed. For which of the following designs will he have enough timber?

Looking at this problem your child should in the first case be able to determine that $10 + 6 \times 2$ is 32 meters, so the carpenter will be able to make a border.

In the second case, she should solve the situation by multiplying 6 times 5 to arrive at 30 meters and decide that the carpenter will also be able to put a border around this garden and will have 2 meters of wood left over. He might use the leftover wood to start a fire to prepare hotdogs to celebrate his new perimeter!

In the third case, the child will have to remember the rules of hypotenuses to determine that since the angled side will be longer than 6 meters, there will not be enough wood to put a border around this garden bed. (If he is creative, maybe he can fill in with a few bricks at the corners.)

Success in transferring information and skills is influenced by the similarity between the original circumstances of learning and the nature of the new situation where transfer is to be demonstrated. The higher the degree of similarity, the greater the possibility of successful transfer. But similarity is not always available.

If what is being learned is a procedure (e.g., addition), the improved and transferred performance will be evaluated primarily through increased speed and better accuracy of results. If the learning is some form of image, symbol, or depiction, the proof of transfer will be through the accuracy of the representation (see figure 7.2).

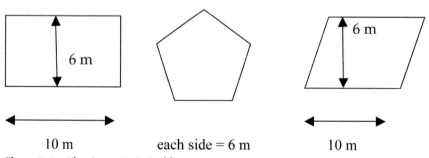

Figure 7.1.   The Carpenter's Problem

To further help understand transfer, let us look at a few examples of factors that stimulate or inhibit transfer. First is what is learned. The degree of specificity of what is learned is a factor in transfer. Look at the range below, which starts with something quite specific and extends to something more abstract:

Mice versus rats → Mammals versus → Biology versus
nonmammals botany

Comparing mice and rats is much more specific than comparing mammals and nonmammals. Comparing biology and botany is even more general. The degree of similarity and specificity will influence the ability to transfer (small cars vs. big trucks).

Another example is *where* the knowledge or skills were learned. As we have emphasized, new skills and knowledge are learned in the classroom but must be used outside the classroom. Can something learned in the classroom be transferred to the playground or to the home?

Classroom → Playground → Home

Place and context can clearly influence the possibilities of transfer.

Time of learning is also a factor that affects the feasibility of transfer. The closer in time between initial learning and transfer, the higher the

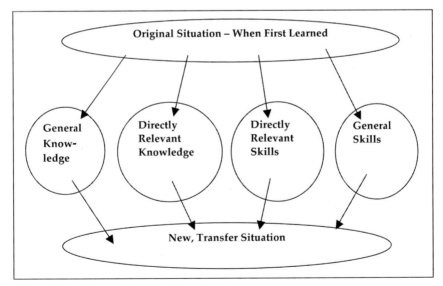

Figure 7.2. A General Model of Transfer

probability of success. If too much time passes between initial learning and the transfer experience, success will be reduced:

Same class session   →   Next day   →   Weeks later

The social context of learning is also important. What an individual learns is specific to him. What is learned in a group may be stronger or weaker, depending on the circumstances of learning. The larger the group, the higher the potential for less direct engagement in learning:

Individual   →   Small group   →   Large group

Finally, the modality of the learned knowledge or skills is an important factor. Any major change in modality will reduce the success of transfer:

Both written   →   Multiple choice   →   Practical application
                         versus essay

If the student learns math through written exercises he will be able to transfer most easily to other similar written exercises. A change to responding to multiple choice questions will require more transfer and a change to practical applications will require even more transfer.

PROBLEM SOLVING

There are also several perspectives from which people solve problems. For example, some people have an idealistic perspective, meaning that they try to solve the problem within a framework of ideals and values, usually of a religious or political nature. Other people solve problems from a practical or pragmatic perspective, emphasizing the realistic results of problem solving. Also, many people use an analytic framework, a systematic perspective that we amplify below. The most widely used approach is the combination of an analytic approach and an idealistic perspective.

Now I present two typical forms of problem solving. I want to emphasize that they are forms which do *not* conform to the expectations of critical thinking approaches. By definition, they are non–critical-thinking approaches, particularly the intuitive mode of problem solving.

TRIAL AND ERROR

Trial and error means discovering the best way to reach a correct solution by trying out one or more ways or means and by noting and eliminating errors or causes of failure. It is a widely used form of problem solving but also the second-least efficient.

The basic approach is to look at the problem and try any idea to solve it. If the first idea does not work, try another idea and so on until you either solve the problem or get tired and move on to something else. It would appear that this form of problem solving is part of our genetic makeup; that is, it derives from thousands of years of evolution because it is simple and precedes more serious thought. All of us use it at one time or another, particularly when confronted with some new situation that we do not fully understand and for which we cannot locate a scheme in our long-term memory. Trial and error is usually good for problems where you have multiple chances to get the correct solution and time is not an important factor. It is not a good technique for problems that don't give you numerous possibilities to find a solution.

Examples of situations where you would not want to use trial and error are diffusing a bomb, performing an operation on a patient, or driving a car. In these situations, making an error can lead to disaster. You would not go to a dentist who uses trial and error to solve your dental problems (although I have my suspicions about some of my past dentists!). Trial and error is used best when it is applied to situations that give you large amounts of time and safety to come up with a solution.

Sometimes trial and error can be a good way to gain knowledge. A person who uses the trial-and-error method will try an idea to see if it is a good solution. If it is not, they try another option. If the method works, the person using it has acquired the correct solution to a problem.

Keep in mind that the purpose of trial and error is not to find out *why* a problem was solved. It is used to solve the problem. While trial and error may be excellent for finding solutions to mechanical or engineering problems, it may not be good for certain fields that require showing knowledge about "why" a solution works.

Many math teachers encourage using trial and error to find a solution to problems, and many of them don't spend a whole lot of time explaining "why" a solution works. One reason for this is because most math teachers have major time constraints in class. This means that some students have to take advanced math classes after school or in college in order to learn more about why certain solutions work. Trial and error is used primarily to find a single solution to a single problem, typically when emphasis is on memorization versus understanding.

Trial and error is not a method of finding the best solution, nor is it a method of finding all solutions. It is a problem-solving technique that is simply used to find a solution. One of the most interesting advantages to this technique is that it does not require your child to have a lot of knowledge. It may require large amounts of patience, and it is not true critical thinking.

INTUITIVE PROBLEM SOLVING

Most of our judgments and actions are governed by intuitive thought. Most of our mental life is relatively effortless. The ease of access with which thoughts come to mind has an influence that almost defines intuition and influences the operations of computation. Our ability to avoid errors depends on what comes to mind and whether the correct thought comes to mind adequately. Intuition means to arrive at conclusions or to make decisions that are instantaneous as opposed to "reasoning" that proceeds in multiple steps. This is common, everyday thinking.

Look at this example, and listen to your intuition:

A bat and a ball cost $1.10.
The bat costs one dollar more than the ball.
How much does the ball cost?

The number that comes to your mind is 10: 10 cents. More than 50 percent of Harvard, MIT, and Princeton university students gave the intuitive—incorrect—answer. Most people do not take the trouble to think through the question. If you answer the question systematically, you will realize that if the ball cost 10 cents, that would be only 90 cents more than the bat. The ball costs 5 cents![1]

In thinking and, in particular, intuition, we do not use all the information that is available. Intuitive activities are similar to perceptual activities, such as seeing and hearing. And some human intuition is good, while some is erroneous. Intuitive impressions come to mind without explicit intention and without any confrontation, and this is one of their distinctive aspects.

Intuitions that experts have make them able to deal swiftly and decisively with difficult matters that would seem to require extensive deliberation, such as making a quick chess move, fighting a fire, or determining when to buy and sell stocks. Most of the time, a person with expert intuition is not really conscious of making a decision but rather acts as though her instinctive choice is the only natural outcome of a circumstance. How she reacts apparently sometimes comes automatically from having large amounts of relevant knowledge structures and extensive experience.

This is not the case of young students who are just learning new subjects. However, unless certain conditions of expertise are fulfilled, such as prolonged practice and rapid feedback, what your child develops is basic knowledge and experience, which can lead to false impressions and overconfidence. Then we find a great deal of self-reliance in the presence of poor accuracy, so the confidence that people have is not a good indication of how accurate they are.

Overconfidence is accentuated by the failure of people to learn from their mistakes. When something happens that a person has not anticipated, he remains convinced that what he had predicted, although it didn't happen, almost happened. This confirmation bias is an important and dangerous misperception.

Beliefs also often depend on intuitive knowledge. Sometimes this is the same as behaving intuitively. Deciding that it is safe to cross the street can be seen as an action we take when there is no traffic, but it also involves the belief that there are no cars that are likely to hit us. This example shows clearly the influence of experience. Young children are much less likely to be aware of the danger of approaching vehicles than are older persons.

The point of responsible thinking is to recognize when intuitive beliefs might be faulty. Some of the reasons they often are faulty include the following:

- Flawed, incomplete, and incorrect information.
- Responding too quickly to inaccurate, insufficient, unreliable, or incomplete information.
- Lack of adequate underlying mental structures.
- Short-term emotional bias; even experts' decisions are influenced by unrelated or irrelevant emotions at the time of making a decision.
- Insufficient consideration of alternatives since intuition relies on pattern recognition and will favor solutions that in the past worked well with the current perceived pattern, which will limit consideration of new options, particularly when dealing with new situations that may require novel or unique solutions.
- Prejudices which help form our intuition and can allow flawed experiences to overrule sound facts and evidence.
- Inappropriate application of solutions since good experience and expertise and intuition in one area can become overconfidence and lead to applying intuition in an unfamiliar or unrelated area (incorrect or inadequate transfer).

For the most part, intuition works well for simple decisions, and we could never get through life without making lots of immediate judgments about the things around us and how we should respond to them. It would be impractical to replace all intuitive judgments by careful logical reasoning, and most of the time it wouldn't give us any better answers than we get intuitively. If we could not use intuition, our world would be slow, laborious, difficult, and costly. The alternative to thinking intuitively is mental paralysis.

We must learn to identify situations in which intuition is liable to lead us astray. What you should do is to help your child develop one more intuitive skill—that of recognizing when a situation is one that commonly fools people, such as when there is an emotional difference of opinion, when someone has something to gain by persuading us of something, or when an extremely rare but sensational mishap occurs. It is in these situations that it pays to attempt to employ careful reasoning to reduce the chances of reaching a false answer or adopting a false belief.

THE SYSTEMATIC OR ANALYTIC
APPROACH TO CRITICAL THINKING

This is the most widely studied and used approach to problem solving. It is the application of the scientific method to the resolution of problems; therefore, it has a good pedigree. Many people say that the analytical approach to problem solving is the essence of critical thinking. That is true. When we approach a problem from an analytic standpoint, we are thinking rationally and in an organized fashion. We are applying solid criteria to our work, especially logic, accuracy, and clarity. We are putting our thinking process and its results to empirical tests of adequacy.

The analytical approach is superior to trial and error because it uses specific methods to increase the probability of success. It is superior to the use of intuition because it is much less distorted by bias and prejudice and does not run as high a risk of failure as does intuition.

The analytic approach to problem solving is usually broken down into a series of steps. Some authors suggest four steps, others as many as 13. For example, the famous mathematician Georg Polya[2] proposed four steps:

1. Understand the problem.
2. Devise a plan.
3. Carry out the plan.
4. Look back (reflect about what worked and what did not).

Polya elaborated each of his four steps into lists of specific actions a problem solver should consider. John Dewey proposed a seven-point problem-solving plan[3] that is similar to the one we suggest. The most typical approach is six steps, as follows:

1. Identify the problem as clearly as possible.
2. Generate criteria and consider possible alternatives for a solution.
3. Choose the most likely alternative solution to the problem.
4. Test or apply the selected strategy.
5. Evaluate progress toward the solution of the problem through feedback.
6. Verify and confirm the effectiveness of the alternative in solving the problem.

This approach to solving problems is inductive. It is often used in activities that start with a hypothesis, as in the cases of math and science. This approach, used with lots of practice, can easily become a cognitive strategy for general and specific problem solving. While presented above as a list of steps, in practice the process will be more fluid, a back-and-forth one, as shown in figure 7.3.

Many approaches to problem solving tend to emphasize mathematics as the key subject area. In fact, both math and reading are areas where problems need to be solved, as are the science subjects, history, and social studies. In our discussion here, we place most emphasis on reading and math as constituting the most crucial areas of school learning.

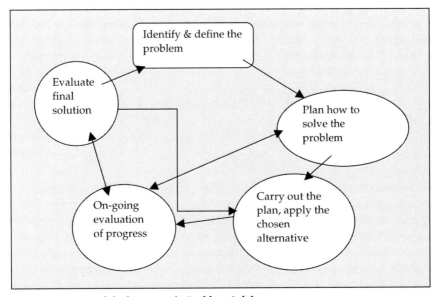

Figure 7.3. A Model of Systematic Problem Solving

IDENTIFY AND UNDERSTAND THE PROBLEM

One of the most important steps involved in problem solving is understanding the problem. While this may seem like a commonsense observation, it is the primary mistake made by people who encounter a problem. Many people who are not well acquainted with analytic problem solving do not study the problem but just charge ahead and try to solve it (often by trial and error—remember the problem of the bat and the ball).

The first step in this approach is to understand the problem. Einstein said that a problem well defined is a problem half solved. He was right, but defining the problem may be more difficult than it might appear. Posing the problem is a challenge, and getting a firm grasp on the nature of the problem is a major step toward its solution. There is empirical research that demonstrates that posing a problem heightens the students' perception of the subject and produces excitement and motivation.

Look again at the problem of the bat and the ball:

A bat and a ball cost $1.10
The bat costs one dollar more than the ball.
How much does the ball cost?

Careful analysis of the problem would stop you or your child from jumping to the intuitive conclusion. What is the problem?

Another example is this one:

A bus starts its route down Main Street. At 1st and Main, it picks up 10 passengers. At 2nd and Main, it picks up three more passengers. At 3rd and Main, two passengers get off, and three get on. At 4th and Main, five passengers get on, and two get off.

At this point, most children will be adding and subtracting the number of passengers. They are trying to solve without paying attention to the question, which is the following:

How many times did the bus stop?

Of course, that is a trick question, but it is used here specifically to demonstrate that one must be sure she understands what is the problem to be solved, that is, what is the question. Your child should ask what will be the questions before starting to solve the problem.

One way to teach problem identification to your child is through what is called problem posing, which improves students' thinking, problem-solving skills, attitudes, and confidence in mathematics.

First steps include asking the following:

- Do you understand all of the words, terms, and concepts presented in the problem?
- Do you understand what you are supposed to demonstrate or be able to do?
- Do you think you have enough information to help you solve the problem, or is more information needed?

One of the problems with learning math in school is that the teacher and the text usually tell the student what to do and do not teach them how to examine problems: "Add these numbers, divide these numbers, and solve for X."

Teaching students how to consider problems is valuable. For example, instead of saying, "Alex has 180 pencils while Chris has 25 pencils more than Alex. How many pencils do both have?," a better way might be to say, "Write a question such that the answer to the problem is 385." That requires your child to examine the various ways the problem can be stated, to choose the operations, and to verify the results.

Help your child ask questions that may lead to clarifying the problem, such as the following:

- What is causing the problem?
- Where is the problem?
- What do I need to explore in order to understand the problem?
- Write a problem based on a chart or a picture.
- Write a problem based on a story.

If your child doesn't understand a problem, he will not be able to solve it. If you are having trouble solving a problem, this means that you probably don't understand it, or you are looking at it from the wrong angle. If you are a math student, changing the way you approach a problem will likely allow you to solve it correctly. One of my favorite examples of changing approach can be seen in this example from third-grade math:

A ship is traveling from Africa to the United States. It carries jungle animals for a zoo.
The ship has seven lions, three elephants, six giraffes, and two rhinoceroses.
How old is the captain of the ship?

Note that the student must figure out which mathematical operation is required. He is not told to add or subtract or to multiply or divide. He must figure that out. Then he has four numbers with which to work. Sometimes younger students add the lions and giraffes to come up with the somewhat romantic idea that the captain is a young person like them. But usually, after only a little manipulation, students realize that the most logical answer is to multiply the number of lions times the number of giraffes to get a logical age for the captain.

Look at this problem:

> My Mom said I could have all the nickels and dimes in her purse. The total of money in her purse is $1.35. How many nickels and dimes do I have?

If asked to define the problem, will your child realize that there may be several possible answers? Can you prompt him to think of alternatives? Here the alternatives require division by 10, division by five, and then a study of the various combinations that will lead to the various correct answers. Can you help him see that the answers can range from 27 nickels to 13 dimes and one nickel and other variations?

A similar problem is the following:

> There are 30 legs in my backyard, counting dogs and children. How many dogs and children are in my backyard?

Again, if asked to define the problem, will the child realize that there may be several possible answers? Can you prompt him to think of alternatives? They can range from seven dogs and one child to 13 children and one dog. Will your child realize that? Knowing these possibilities is a basic part of being able to understand problems.

READING AND PROBLEM SOLVING

Problems are often found in reading stories and literature. Fully understanding texts, being able to apply their information to everyday situations, and predicting certain events based on text information are all problems to be solved through text comprehension and analysis.

There are three main types of problem solving in reading. The first is summarizing. After reading a story, an expository text, an article, or a chapter, the question is to what degree the reader can adequately summarize what has been read. Is your child able to identify the important information and to link it in a meaningful series or pattern (first this, then this, and then this result)?

- Can she create a time line or a concept map for the story?
- Can she identify the more important words from the less important ones?
- Can she find the topic sentence?

In a problem-solving sequence, your child should be able to find the most important pattern in the information and identify the less important elements. That is the nature of the problem to be solved when summarizing. This activity is much like paraphrasing but on a bigger scale. Accuracy is important.

The second problem is inference. Can your child draw the appropriate inferences from the material that has been read? Why do readers make inferences when they read? A reader's mind is always trying to make sense of what it is encountering. This is consistent with our concept of learning: encountering, assimilating, and adapting ideas, concepts, and so on into new structures. Remember the emphasis placed on developing skills of inference (chapter 3).

The third problem-related skill is prediction. Given a unit of reading material (story, text, chapter, and so on), can your child make predictions of what will occur next when stopped during the reading of the text? Prediction consists of forming expectations regarding what will happen next in a story or anticipating what the author of an expository text will say next.

As your child reads, she must determine which problem she is confronting. Often there is a natural sequence: summarizing, inferring, and predicting.

GENERATE ALTERNATIVES FOR THE SOLUTION

If your child has been able to state or describe the nature of the problem and what is being asked for, then she should be able to develop some ideas about how to solve it. Look at this problem:

> Matt is going on a walk-a-thon. For every half mile he walks, he will get 75 cents. When he finished his walk, he had $3.75. How far did he walk?

If she has understood the problem, then she should be able to identify that division is the correct method for solving the problem.

What is the best approach to this problem?

> George gets an allowance every day. On Monday he gets one cent, on Tuesday he gets two cents, on Wednesday he gets three cents, on Thursday he gets four cents, and so on. How much money will he have by the 12th day? By the 16th day?

What kind of alternatives can be generated? One is to simply add the amounts for each day until achieving the answer. Another is to multiply the day by one cent and add all of the results.

In the generation of possible solutions to problems, one technique that is widely recommended is "brainstorming," trying to think of as many possible solutions without putting excessive limits on what solutions are allowed. This is usually a group problem-solving technique that involves the spontaneous contribution of ideas from all members of the group, but it can also be the mulling over of ideas by one or more individuals in an attempt to devise or find a solution to a problem. You and your child together can brainstorm as you guide and lead the process at first.

Remember the basic structure of a story (see figure 7.4). In the analysis of a story, the initial setting introduces the hero, sets his goals (or his problem), and describes the basic context or environment within which he is to solve the problem. The reader assumes that the central character will follow a rational plan to meet his goal.

All this provides much information to the reader, your child, so the generation of solution alternatives will most likely be based on the rational plan. The problem for your child is not to create a plan but to recognize the plan that will be followed by the protagonist of the story. In helping her solve that problem, you will remind her of what is the problem and suggest that she look at the various events of the story and how they help the hero to work toward a solution.

Often you can prompt your child to think of situations or events in her own background that may help understand the path to a solution with questions such as the following:

Remember when we had that . . . ?
What happened when Daddy had a . . . ?
What did Grandmother do when . . . ?

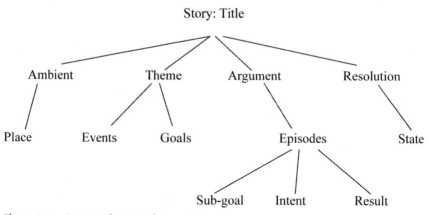

Figure 7.4. Structural Network For a Story

When interpreting fables, parables, legends, or myths, the interpretive or predictive elements become more clear. When reading an expository text, is your child required to summarize the text (a common situation) or determine cause and effect and/or predict some future event on the basis of the reading?

The general guideline is to stimulate or evoke relevant background knowledge ("remember when . . ."); ask your child to explain, infer, and predict during reading ("think out loud . . ."); and then ask inferential questions after finishing reading.

Look at this example:

A group of students went on a camping trip with their families. They spotted a cave on the side of a hill and decided to explore it. All of the adults except one went into the cave to make sure it would be safe for the children to enter. Just after the adults entered, a large boulder dislodged from above and fell over the entrance of the cave so that the adults could not get out.

What has happened? What is the problem? How big is the boulder? How many children are there? How might the problem be solved? Who has a cell phone?

CHOOSE THE MOST LIKELY ALTERNATIVE SOLUTION TO THE PROBLEM

Remember the ship with zoo animals? The students had several options, including four functions and four numbers. They had to decide which function would come up with the most reasonable answer. They had to choose the most likely alternative. In math problems, your child will have to identify which functions are required to develop a solution to the problem.

In choosing alternatives for identifying the plan of the protagonist in a story, your child will most likely compare the story to other stories she has heard and read and will try to identify similarities between them and the current story in order to increase the probability of identifying the protagonist's plan.

TEST OR APPLY THE SELECTED ALTERNATIVE OR STRATEGY

Having chosen what appears to be the optimal alternative to arrive at a solution, your child should apply it in the process that will lead to a result.

Here is a math example:

My mom said I could have all the nickels and dimes in her purse. The total of money in her purse is $1.35. How many nickels and dimes do I have?

The alternative is one that requires multiple divisions (by 5 and by 10) and the generation of options that will respond adequately to the problem.

EVALUATE PROGRESS TOWARD THE SOLUTION OF THE PROBLEM THROUGH FEEDBACK

This is particularly important for longer and more complex problems but can also be applied to less complex ones. For example, the two math word problems mentioned above that had multiple potential answers would require that the child constantly evaluate progress toward a solution. Is she identifying all the options available in the solution? Is she applying the correct math functions? Are the results accurate and correct? Is she progressing adequately in terms of time; that is, is she taking too much or too little time to solve the problem?

In the case of understanding the story, your child's hypothesis about the plan of the protagonist will be compared to the progress of the story, and at some point she will decide if her hypothesis is right or if it needs to be modified or changed. Is she identifying the most important aspects of the story? Can she create a story line—a clear summary of the story? Can she explain why the resolution is logical and solves the problem? And is she doing all this within the expected time frame?

VERIFY AND CONFIRM THE EFFECTIVENESS OF THE ALTERNATIVE IN SOLVING THE PROBLEM

Your child will want to know if her responses are correct. If she is working directly with you, it will be possible for you to provide immediate confirmation. If she is doing homework, the worksheets have to go to school to be seen by the teacher. Getting feedback from the teacher can often be a long process.

Immediate feedback is useful in the early stages of learning. Parents can provide confirmation in the early stages, but you should also start to teach your child how to do self-confirmation of his answers, for example, by resubtracting addition problems or by multiplying division problems:

```
 427       5382       2853
+367      +  425      +3471
 794       5807        6324
-367      -  425      -2853
 427       5382        3471
```

A FEW MORE EXAMPLES OF PROBLEM SOLVING

Emily's aunt gave her $125 to spend on clothes at the mall (see table 7.1). She bought four blouses that cost $18 each and a pair of pants that cost $22. How much money does she have left?

Your mother baked a batch of blueberry muffins (see table 7.2). There are 16 muffins in each batch. Your mother ate one-fourth of the batch. Then she baked two more batches. How many muffins does she have?

This simple step-by-step approach to problem solving, if used starting in first or second grade and continued thereafter for a few years, will develop a cognitive strategy of systematic problem solving for your child. This strategy will last a lifetime.

Table 7.1. Emily's Money

Identify the problem	How much money left after purchases.	
Generate alternatives	Addition, multiplication, and subtraction.	Multiply 18 × 4 Add to the above sum 22
Choose most likely alternative	Add the costs of the items Subtract from the original amount.	
Apply the alternative	Add and subtract.	Multiply 18 × 4 Add to the above sum 22 Subtract from 125
Evaluate progress	During progress, check to see that the sum of the amount of clothes purchased is correct before subtracting it from the original amount.	18 × 4 = ____ 72 + 22 = ____ 125 − 94 = ____
Confirm effectiveness	Take the final amount and add it to the value of the purchased goods to see if it equals the amount Emily's aunt gave.	Final answer was $31 Confirmation by adding 72 + 22 + 31 to equal 125

Table 7.2.   Mother's Blueberry Muffins

Identify the problem	How many muffins.	
Generate alternatives	Addition, multiplication, division, and subtraction.	Multiply 16 × 3 Divide 16 by one-fourth Subtract one-fourth from the result of 16 × 3
Choose most likely alternative	Determine the total number of muffins prepared. Subtract one-fourth of one batch.	
Apply the alternative	Multiply, divide, and subtract.	Multiply 16 × 3 Divide 16 by one-fourth Subtract one-fourth from the result of 16 × 3
Evaluate progress	During progress, check to see that the sum of the three batches is correct. Check that the result of one-fourth of 16 is correct.	What is 16 × 3? What is one-fourth of 16?
Confirm effectiveness	Take the final amount and add to it the number of muffins Mother ate.	Final answer was 44 Confirmation by adding 44 + 4 to get amount of three batches

MAKING MISTAKES

To successfully solve problems, your child will need to be able to deal with failure. The way she handles mistakes must be taken into consideration. If she gives up after making mistakes, she will not solve the problem. If she keeps trying, she will eventually find a solution that can allow her to overcome any problem. People who are good at solving problems aren't afraid of making mistakes. They will continue making mistakes until they find a solution.

The most important part of making a mistake is learning from it. Mistakes can provide a foundation that will allow you to solve a problem that you may encounter in the future. The second thing that you will need to overcome is frustration. This is easier said than done. When people run into a problem that is difficult to solve, they will often become frustrated. This is especially true if the solutions they've come up with have failed. Allowing frustration to take over will cause your child to lose focus.

Frustration will hinder your child from solving problems. Because of this, you should teach her to be as calm as possible when she attempts to overcome a problem that is challenging. When Josephine gets frustrated, sometimes with the piano work and sometimes with her sports games,

I use calm and encouraging language, rub her shoulders, give her some hugs, and similar things, all the while using soothing language and reassurances that I know she can solve her sports problem or finish her piano piece. I place more emphasis on effort than on talent: "You can do it if you try hard!"

After your child has solved a problem, it is also important to make a note of how she solved it. This can be a mental or a physical note.

The provision of constancy is a primary role of parents. When your child shows signs of frustration, you must remind him that he is capable, that he will be able to solve the problem (ability), and that the key to solving it is persistence and hard work.

CREATIVITY AND INTUITION

Given that creativity is somewhat difficult to define, it is not surprising that there are many conflicting explanations of it. The problem is not so much how to explain originality as how to explain how some people have it, even become experts at it, and can produce works that are clearly creative while so many others cannot.

Creativity and talent are two ideas to explain phenomena and results that are not easy to explain. The big danger with these terms is that they can be—and often are—circular. How do you know if a person has talent? Because he does something rather extraordinary, like becoming a chess master at the age of 13. But in this case, we are simply using the term *talent* to explain what we have seen. He is a chess master at 13; therefore, he has talent. A famous writer devoted a book to the idea that great performance requires about 10,000 hours of practice, but he could not explain why some people (like swimmers and soccer players) could achieve outstanding performance in only 2,000 hours or less. Was that talent?

Creativity is similar: We know it when we see it, but we do not know to what it might be credited; where does it come from? Since I have a major inclination toward music, I usually think of Bach, Beethoven, and Mozart as great examples of creativity, with a major sort of independence of imagination, as exemplified in their works. Mozart thought that it was a gift given to him by God. So did Bach, but a careful study of Bach's background shows that he was a conscientious worker who studied counterpoint assiduously for many years.

Three main factors are involved. The first is innate intelligence, over which parents have little control. The second is the depth of knowledge the child has, an issue over which parents can have much control. The third is willingness to explore, to reconceptualize, to shift perspective, and to change the framing of the issue, which is a complicated skill but over which parents also have considerable influence.

Since we have rather limited control over innate intelligence, the main lesson is to identify it, stimulate it as much as possible, and try to create circumstances where intelligence can become fruitful (motivate and create positive dispositions).

That takes us to the second point, which is that most creativity is a result of high levels of expertise in some domain, that is, very well structured information about a subject that is mastered in depth, providing a basis from which ingenious, imaginative, and resourceful products can emerge.

The development of expertise takes much time and effort, and it often is easier for some children than it is for others. For example, one study showed that people can become chess masters in as little as 3,000 hours of practice even though the normal average time to become a master is in excess of 11,000 hours, and some people take as long as 23,000 hours to achieve that level. Individual differences exist and are important.

Risk taking is related to expertise and also to the way children approach problems. If your child is good at analytical thinking, that will be a major help in achieving a good level of knowledge and expertise. But creativity usually arises from synthetic thinking (which is not incompatible with analytical thinking but which also is not generally taught).

Synthetic thinking is the process of putting things together by combining the parts that go to make those things up: A + B + C + D equals a result. A, B, C, and D are ideas that are brought together to produce a particular product or result. When those ideas are brought together often, we come up with an idea that transcends any of these four parts that went to make it up.

This bringing together is the process of synthesis. In the realm of thoughts and ideas, a number of concepts are combined to synthesize an idea whose whole is in some sense greater than simply the sum of its parts. By combining the partial ideas, we achieve something that we did not have when those partial ideas were separated. This could be thought of as analogous to a real-world example wherein we bring together lettuce, tomatoes, carrots, celery, and onions to make a salad. The parts that make up the salad do not constitute a salad until we bring them together.

Synthesis is different than analysis, which is the process of conceptually breaking something down into its component parts or ingredients. In this sense, analysis could be thought of as the opposite of synthesis. The analysis methods we saw above usually start from a central main idea that is divided into smaller units, often organized hierarchically. The process of synthetic thinking is more a matter of starting at the extremities and moving in toward the center. Synthesis allows us to construct a whole salad out of its parts. Analysis allows us to conceptually break down something into the parts that it could be made of.

Both analysis and synthesis are useful. Certainly your child should have both of these intellectual tools available, not only one or the other. Figuring out what went wrong is likely to be a matter of analysis. Figuring out how we can make things better in the future is a matter of synthesis. Problem solving is usually a matter of analysis. Creativity is a matter of synthesis.

The best way to help your child develop more synthetic thinking and therefore more potential for creativity is through emphasis on comparison and contrast. These activities help your child learn to combine presumably disparate units into something new.

A major concept in the growth of structured learning and critical thinking is *development*. Your child will develop the ability to think critically over a period of years and in doing so will go through stages of progress. Mental development does not happen overnight. It is a slow process, but if done correctly, it can go faster than what might be normal (e.g., if you trusted the school to do the work).

By starting with a clear idea of how your child learns and then helping him develop cognitive strategies and metacognition for better and more effective learning and by stimulating good intellectual standards and encouraging positive attitudes toward learning and persistence, you will significantly enhance your child's overall intellectual and emotional ability. Table 7.3 shows how the developmental process for solving problems will likely advance, what you can expect, and what you should reinforce.

Table 7.3. The Developmental Process for Problem-Solving

Strategy	3 to 5 years	6 to 8 years	9 to 11 years	12+
Basic recovery	Most emphasis is on ensuring effectiveness of learning as evidenced by recovery.	Continuation of learning effectiveness and reliable recovery.	Continuation of learning effectiveness and reliable recovery.	While recovered content becomes more complex, the strategy should be well established.
Simple application	Through improved speaking ability and initial development of number concepts.	Major growth of verbal and mathematical concepts and skills.	Continued major growth of verbal and mathematical concepts and skills.	Complexity of application ability should be growing.
Transfer	Simple transfer experiences may be taught.	Transfer activities should grow in verbal skills (reading, speaking, and writing) and in math concepts and skills.	Ability to transfer should improve in verbal skills and in math concepts and skills.	The strategy of transfer should be well developed and reliable, although content demands may be more complex.
Problem solving	Incipient problem solving through games and physical activities.	Problem solving in math and verbal areas should be growing quickly.	Problem solving in math and verbal areas should continue to grow quickly.	The ability to solve problems in relevant domains (math, language, physical skills, and so on) should be well developed.
Creativity	Incipient evidence.	Some creativity may be seen in verbal and visual areas.	More creativity may be seen in verbal and visual areas and in math.	This is a period when more creativity should be expected, although it may still be rudimentary.

EIGHT

High-Quality Critical Thinking: Wrapping Up

High Quality Thinking!
Wrapping Up

Teaching critical thinking is complex, as we have seen. There are five major elements involved, and each of these has a series of essential components that contribute to the overall objective.

We have examined all five components in some detail, and as a parent you should be able to teach them to your children. It will not always be easy: There are many elements, they require much repetition over a period of many months, and your child may not always catch on as quickly as you desire. Remember the disposition called persistence: If you want your child to think critically, you will have to be very persistent (and consistent).

The constellation of concepts, events, knowledge, skills, attitudes, and dispositions and standards required for critical thinking have been outlined in this book in such a manner that, it is hoped, you understand them and feel convinced that these suggestions offer a feasible road to the development of critical thinking in your children and are worth investing time and effort in them (see figure 8.1).

Following the guidelines we have presented in this book will lead your child to have a solid base of knowledge that is well organized and well structured and not a haphazard, loosely organized bunch of "stuff" in her head—knowledge that is easy to expand on, easy to recover, and easy to transfer to new situations. Your child will also have cognitive skills to significantly facilitate the learning and retention of new information and the metacognitive awareness that will allow her to know when she is making progress, when she is not, when she is sure of mastery, and when more effort is required. With consistent and constant help, your child will develop positive attitudes toward learning and knowledge based on the gratifying sense of self-effectiveness—having the knowledge and the assurance that she can learn and do things that are useful, important, and satisfying.

You will have a child, going into the teenage years, who is able to access, select, and evaluate knowledge from an information-heavy world; decide what to believe or to do; provide evidence in support of one's suggestion or conclusions and ask for evidence from others before accepting their conclusions; and determine the authenticity, accuracy, meaningfulness, and value of information. You will have a child who knows how to use skills and strategies that will increase the likelihood of achieving desired outcomes as determined by the thinker and being able to make good career decisions, astute financial decisions, and general life decisions—a child who will think purposefully, reasonably, and in a goal-directed fashion, directed toward solving problems, deducing inferences, calculating probabilities, and making decisions.

AND THERE IS MORE

Your child not only will think critically but also will likely enjoy learning and achieving. Through the process of learning to think critically, he will become a self-sufficient learner, one who enjoys learning and the feeling of self-efficacy and the joys of discovery. He will be able to do the following:

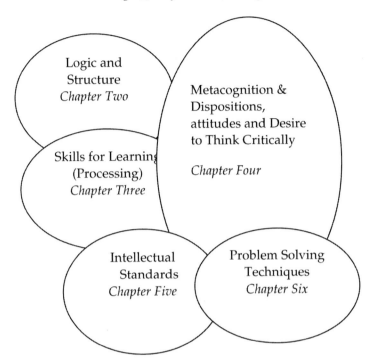

Figure 8.1. The Model for Critical Thinking

- Know how to set goals for himself and keep track of daily progress
- Will approach educational tasks with confidence, diligence, and resourcefulness
- Will be aware of when he knows a concept or fact and when he masters a skill and when he does not and will adjust his behavior accordingly
- Will be able to set, organize, and self-monitor his learning at various points during the process
- Will be able to select, structure, and create environments that optimize learning
- Will use metacognitive, motivational, and behavioral strategies in a systematic manner

Learners who are self-motivated and self-regulated will be able to do the following:

- Practice, repeat, and review what they learn as often as necessary
- Have a deliberate intention of learning new ideas and skills
- Learn in a systematic way, not haphazardly
- Perceive and correct their errors quickly

Your child then becomes a serious learner who understands that while talent is useful, the best approach is to emphasize effort and that doing so can boost intelligence. She will realize that people become more intelligent through sustained and targeted effort and that they can achieve much more than they normally would anticipate—that intelligence develops over time by solving hard problems and working on challenges until they achieve what they desire. They will have learned that positive effort creates more intelligence.

Notes

CHAPTER 1

1. Matthew Lipman, *Thinking in Education*, 2nd ed. (New York: Cambridge University Press, 2003).
2. Lipman, *Thinking in Education*.
3. Elena Silva, "Measuring Skills for the 21st Century," November 3, 2008, http://www.educationsector.org/publications/measuring-skills-21st-century.
4. F. Levy and R. Murnane, *Dancing with Robots: Human Skills for Computerized Work*, http://content.thirdway.org/publications/714/Dancing-With-Robots.pdf.
5. Richard Arum and Josipa Roksa, *Academically Adrift: Limited Learning on College Campuses* (Chicago: University of Chicago Press, 2011).
6. Center for Educational Reform, *Newswire* 12, no. 31 (August 17, 2010).

CHAPTER 2

1. The importance of schemata for thought cannot be overstated. Sufferers of Korsakov syndrome are unable to form new memories and must approach every situation as if they had just seen it for the first time. Many sufferers adapt by continually forcing their world into barely applicable schemata, often to the point of incoherence and self-contradiction.
2. Process concepts represent mechanisms of evaporation, condensation, photosynthesis, or an atomic reaction.
3. D. N. Perkins and T. A. Grotzer, "Teaching Intelligence," *American Psychologist* 52, no. 10 (1997): 1125–33.
4. Interest in the structure of disciplines also has a long history. For example, J. J. Schwab (*The Teaching of Science: The Teaching of Science as Enquiry* [Cambridge, MA: Harvard University Press, 1962]) claimed that he and his colleagues had taught a course on it for the first time in 1941. According to P. H. Phenix "Key Concepts and the Crisis in Learning," *Teachers College Record* (1956) vol. 58, no. 3, 137–43, he, too, had published a paper in 1956 titled "Key Concepts and the Crisis in Learning," in which he advocated paying attention to the "key concepts" in the several fields of learning. The concept of the structure of a discipline became popular through S. Bruner's book *The Process of Education*. (Cambridge, MA: Harvard University Press,

1960). Since then, several countries have developed various curricula based on this structuralist view. The science curricula of the 1960s are good examples.

5. M. Joseph, *The Trivium: The Liberal Arts of Logic, Grammar, and Rhetoric* (Paul Dry Books, 2002).

6. Bruner, *The Process of Education*.

CHAPTER 3

1. Robert Service, "The Cremation of Sam McGee," http://www.wordinfo.info/words/index/info/view_unit/2640/?letter=C&spage=26 (an outstanding example of how sensory stimuli are emphasized, and it has a surprise ending).

2. The listing we give follows the work of R. M. Gagné, *The Conditions of Learning*, 4th ed. (New York: Holt, Rinehart and Winston, 1985); C. E. Weinstein, and V. L. Underwood, "Learning Strategies: The How of Learning," in *Relating Instruction to Basic Research*, J. Segal, S. Chipman, and R. Glaser (Eds.) (Hillsdale, NJ: Lawrence Erlbaum, 1985); R. Stenberg, "Toward a Triarchic Theory of Human Intelligence," Behavior and Brain Sciences (1985), 7, 269–87; and C. Chadwick, "Estrategias Cognitivas y Afectivas en el Aprendizaje" *Revista Latinoamericano de Psicologia* (1988) 20, no. 2, 162–205.

3. See, for example, http://www.brainmetrix.com/memory-game/ or http://www.memory-improvement-tips.com/brain-games.html.

4. http://www.merriam-webster.com/premium/mwunabridged/faq.html.

5. M. C. Wittrock, Carolyn Marks, and Marleen Doctorow, "Reading as a Generative Process," *Journal of Educational Psychology* (1975), vol 67(4), 484–489; and J. Levin, L. Shriberg, G. Miller, C. McCormick, and B. Levin, "The Keyword Method: How to Remember the States and Their Capitals," *The Elementary School Journal* (1980), 185–91; http://cmap.ihmc.us/publications/researchpapers/theorycmaps/theoryunderlyingconceptmaps.htm.

6. Image credit: http://www.123rf.com/photo_12344427_set-of-objects-for-home-work-and-household.html.

7. Image credit: http://www.123rf.com/photo_13496582_dinosaur-cartoon.html.

8. http://cmap.ihmc.us/publications/researchpapers/theorycmaps/theoryunderlyingconceptmaps.htm.

9. http://en.wikipedia.org/wiki/Olympic_Games.

10. Edward N. Zalta, principal ed., *The Stanford Encyclopedia of Philosophy*, http://plato.stanford.

11. http://www.kidbibs.com/learningtips/lt26.htm.

12. J. A. Glover, R. R. Ronning, and R. H. Bruning, *Cognitive Psychology and Instruction* (Englewood Cliffs, NJ: Prentice Hall, 1990).

13. Bruce D. McCandliss, Mindy Kalchman, and Peter Bryant, "Design Experiments and Laboratory Approaches to Learning: Steps toward Collaborative Exchange," *Educational Researcher* 32, no. 1 (2001): 14–16.

CHAPTER 4

1. J. Hattie, *Visible Learning: A Synthesis of Over 800 Meta-Analyses Relating to Achievement* (New York: Routledge, 2008).

CHAPTER 5

1. Peggy Noonan, *Wall Street Journal*, 2001.
2. For a more detailed study, see Robert Nozick, *Invariances: The Structure of the Objective World* (Cambridge, MA: Belknap Press, 2001).
3. Search for "The Little Engine That Could" on the Internet.

CHAPTER 6

1. See http://www.criticalthinking.org.

CHAPTER 7

1. Example from Daniel Kahneman's excellent book *Thinking: Fast and Slow* (New York: Farrar, Strauss and Giroux, 2011).
2. See http://home.comcast.net/~mrtwhs/mash/polya.pdf.
3. See, for example, http://faculty.scf.edu/frithl/SPC1608update/handouts/Dewey.htm.

About the Author

Clifton Chadwick has 40 years of experience helping ministries of education throughout the world (Central and South America, Europe, Asia, Africa, and the Middle East). He is a decisive leader in the development of the concepts of cognitive strategies, metacognition, and affective variables in learning. He has extensive experience in curriculum, evaluation of learning, project evaluation, textbooks and educational materials, educational technology, teacher training, and evaluation.